the next good thing

the

A True Story of

next

Positivity and Transformation

good

in 10 Lessons

thing

Marcos Perez and D. Eric Maikranz

U

**UNION
SQUARE
& CO.**

NEW YORK

UNION
SQUARE
& CO.
NEW YORK

ISBN 978-1-4549-5218-3
ISBN 978-1-4549-5219-0 (e-book)

For information about custom editions, special sales, and premium purchases,
please contact specialsales@unionsquareandco.com.

Printed in the United States of America

2 4 6 8 10 9 7 5 3 1

unionsquareandco.com

Cover design by Elizabeth Mihaltse Lindy
Interior design by Kevin Ullrich

This book is dedicated to our friend Joe Sabah.

You wrote goodness on my heart with your life. You left me without the excuse to ever give up on kindness and the work of loving with all your days. I will keep going with your tenacious heart setting my pace.

Thank you, Joe. I love you.

CHAPTER 1

The email looked ominous. Bold and unread at the top of the inbox, the subject line read: *Stop by my office first thing in the morning.* I felt my stomach drop. It was a follow-up performance review with my new boss, John Gorman, the man who had been criticizing and hounding me and all the older artists at the firm. I took a deep breath and wished that I had not opened the laptop after coming home. *If an email goes unread—can it go unlived?* I wondered as I pushed back in my home office chair. *Is this the beginning of the end at work?*

My mind flashed back to the past year's challenges that had led me to the edge of what now felt like an opening abyss. *Would losing this lifeline of a job send me tumbling down further?* Sometimes when I meditated, it seemed like I could feel the antidepressants that had been in my system for the last year. They had helped me keep it together through it all—calming me, protecting me, but also limiting me in ways I couldn't quite define. Some days I just felt an absence, like something was being silently stolen from me. *Was feeling spacey and losing some creative drive part of being fifty now, or was it because of the antidepressants?* Maybe John was right, maybe I was losing a step to the younger, hungrier artists who kept coming through the door.

Looking around my cluttered basement office, I knew I wouldn't be able to relax with the kids until I read the email. I clicked on it and started reading.

Marcos,

Stop by my office first thing tomorrow morning. We need to discuss your performance and set up an action plan for improvement. Please bring something to take notes on.

John Gorman, Senior Art Director

"An action plan," I repeated as I thought about how to prepare. *What actions can I take to save this job? What actions do I need to take to hold on to this lifeline?* I took my leather journal out of the desk and flipped to the first blank page. I wrote "Action Plan" at the top of the page just as a gentle guitar chord echoed down the stairs to me. It had to be Elliott with my guitar. I listened for a few seconds and then rose from my chair, unable to resist the call of those first slow notes. Walking toward the stairs, I grabbed my ukulele from its case and climbed toward the music.

Elliott stopped when he heard my creaking footsteps cross the hardwood floor, but he moved forward on the old couch as he reset his fingers on the frets and started the song again. I sat in the matching tan chair across from him but didn't raise my instrument to join him. I listened as familiar sad notes echoed in the small living room of our ninety-year-old bungalow home. Elliott played Johnny Cash's acoustic version of "Hurt."

Elliott strummed the strings as Cash's soulful words about hurting himself just to feel something, anything, filled the air between us. My guitar looked so big in his hands. His hair was a black-dyed mess that fell over his left eye and swayed as his head moved. I watched his face and felt the emotion as he played in time with the tapping toe of his heavy black army boot against the floor. He sang in a low voice, lower than I thought he should be able to, as he attuned his heart to the lyrics in a way that highlighted some pain I hadn't recognized before.

I loved connecting with my kids through music. For my youngest daughter, Lilly, it was vintage dance records and learning new ballroom steps. With Elliott, even before the change, it was always playing music together. I was tempted to join in as I squeezed the narrow neck of the ukulele in my hands, but it felt like he was performing the song for me.

I listened to the feeling he put into each word. Should my sixteen-year-old be feeling like this? Was he starting the slide into that familiar darkness again?

"It's in G," Elliott whispered to me as a prompt to join in.

I flipped up my small instrument into a tight cradle and began to strum lightly over the top of his notes as he continued the haunting, melancholic lyrics.

Elliott's tone changed and brightened with the sound of the whimsical ukulele floating over his stronger chords.

Fourteen-year-old Lilly poked her head out of her room to follow our strange song and we eventually drew her out into the living room with us. When we were done, she laughed. "Johnny Cash on the ukulele? I'm not so sure about that one."

"Do you think you can do better?" Elliott challenged through a rare smile.

Lilly reached a thin arm over and grabbed the old concertina I had rescued from a thrift store. It was a fiendishly frustrating thing to play and seemed to be filled with only sour sounds. She snapped open the dried red leather straps and expanded the hexagonal bellows as the instrument drew in a groaning off-key breath. Lilly raised her eyebrows in comic expectation as she pressed a few random keys and squeezed the protesting instrument to life.

I started strumming my ukulele to accompany her enthusiastic noisemaking.

"What are we doing?" Elliott asked above the din.

"Just try anything in C," I shouted as I kept my eyes on Lilly's funny facial expressions that punctuated each moan from her instrument.

Elliott joined in with a few chords that seemed to anchor the chaos for a bit as my daughter droned on. He slowed his playing until we disintegrated back into noise.

"Not bad, not bad at all," I said as I stopped playing.

"Are you kidding me?" Elliott laughed. "That was a train wreck."

Lilly ignored him and just kept squeezing and expanding the poor instrument. "I think I'm getting the hang of it," she shouted with an approving nod over the tortured sounds.

Elliott set down the guitar and grabbed his old band tuba off its rack on the wall. He pointed the open bell toward his sister and blew a loud honk. Lilly wrinkled her nose at the sound and squeezed another discord in Elliott's direction as if answering his challenge.

Back and forth they went, laughing between the offending blasts. I stepped over our confused pug Zuzu and brought out my tarnished old trumpet from the back of the closet.

Elliott's tuba notes had an almost narrative character to them, as if he were arguing with her and the protesting concertina. I raised the trumpet to my lips and joined in the argument with a defiant high note that turned both of their sounds toward me. I slowly lowered my pitch and softened my volume until the cacophony quieted down into a series of sheepish, almost comical, musical apologies. I broke out laughing when I couldn't take my trumpet any lower to meet Elliott's lamenting tuba notes. Elliott and Lilly both started laughing with me at the same time. It was just the fun I needed. Thinking about the action plan would have to wait.

I was afraid as I entered the building. *Will today be my last day? Will I be walking out with my personal items in a box in the next hour? Is there still time to save this job?*

"I need this job," I whispered to myself as I pushed open the glass front door and saw my boss John sitting at this desk with his office door open. He looked up to see me and waved me over.

"Close the door, Marcos," he said as I walked into his office. "How are you?"

"To be honest, I'm feeling a bit nervous about this."

"Marcos, these are not easy for me either, but we have to talk about your performance lately."

I looked at him and nodded.

John paused for a second as though waiting for me. "You might want to write some of this down."

"Oh, right," I said as I fumbled through my canvas rucksack for my journal. *Did this mean I wasn't getting fired today?*

He retrieved a prepared document from his desk drawer and placed it in front of him. "Marcos, this is a performance plan agreement that our HR team provided for us. This will also serve as a written warning"—he paused as he tapped his index finger on the corner of the paper—"and it is also a final warning."

"I understand," I said as I opened my journal and started writing. *Final Warning.*

"Marcos, I have mentioned these items to you on numerous occasions, but I have been instructed that I need to go over them again now as the outline for an action plan that you will define and that I will approve and monitor for improvement. If you do not improve on these performance items, they will be grounds for termination from your role here. Do you understand?"

His words sounded well-practiced, and I got the feeling he had already made up his mind about firing me and this exercise was him just going through the required motions. "Yes, I understand."

"Take this down, please," he said as he looked up and recalled his list of frustrations. "You need to be quicker at returning emails to me, and to the creative directors and account teams."

"I like to block out some time away from emails and distractions in the mornings so that I can focus on the illustrations that are due," I offered but instantly regretted it because I could sense his annoyance that I had interrupted what promised to be a long list of complaints. "Sorry, please continue."

6

"Tardiness is an issue as well, Marcos. You were late to Chris's meeting."

I wanted to reply that I was late because Chris had asked me to wrap up his last-minute additions, but I just felt like getting this over with.

"And then there are a series of what I would call professionalism issues." John paused as though inventorying them. "Your emails to me and the other directors often have spelling mistakes. I have caught several creative description write-ups that contain spelling errors. Marcos, these are client-facing proposals. We can't have this. It's embarrassing."

I wrote down the words as he continued, but I really wanted to crawl between the pages and just pull the leather cover closed over me.

"I feel like your artwork quality is substandard compared to your peers'. And I'm not the only one who feels this way. You need to up your game creatively. I think the last work you did that blew us away was the sports car driving-school campaign."

That was after the divorce, but before my depression diagnosis.

"And then there are other professionalism issues . . . ," he droned on.

I wrote them down one by one, and felt my anxiety rise with each new criticism. *Is it really this bad? Or is he just targeting the older artists to make way for a younger vision now that he's been promoted?*

"Things are different now than when Jordan ran the department. I need more professionalism. It's a reflection on the whole department."

7

"I'm sorry we're at this place, John. It's been a difficult year for me."

John nodded and his face softened a bit. "We all know about your divorce, and Janice in HR told me about the time you took off after your daughter's attempted—"

"Son," I corrected. Getting Elliott's gender right was important after all that we'd been through.

John looked down to double-check his prepared notes for a second before he continued. "Marcos, we want to support you and your family through this, but we must meet these standards that I have detailed for you."

"I think I need to wean myself off the antidepressants I started taking last year," I blurted out. "They make me spacey, and I just feel like I'm off sometimes."

8

"You do what you need to, Marcos. But the items I detailed for you must be corrected. Understood?"

"Yes, it takes a month or two to come off my medication. I hope you can give me that long."

"I don't know what to do with you, Marcos," he said with a sigh. "You can have that long if you improve in these areas right away. I think you should take the rest of the day off to think about your career and draft an action plan to address the items I have detailed for you."

His voice sounded cold and clinical again, as he signed the document and turned it around for me to sign. I closed the journal and signed the document as I thought about Elliott and Lilly and what I would do if I couldn't hang on here.

* * *

I drove straight home, but then sat in the narrow driveway for a long time looking at our small 1930s bungalow. The mortgage payment suddenly seemed so much bigger than the shelter it provided us. *It could be at risk now*, I thought as I gripped the wheel of my one-year-old car—whose payments now felt oversized too.

Entering the house, I went straight to my desk in the basement, sat down in my chair, and started my laptop. The house was quiet, except for the burbling snore of the sleeping pug. This house was never quiet. John was smart to send me home today. With both kids in school, I would have no distractions. I opened a new document and typed the title: *Marcos Perez—Action Plan*.

My mind was still sharp with the shock of the meeting. "What is my Action Plan?" I asked myself out loud.

"Number one, stop being a space cadet," I answered as I typed *Stop Spacing Out*. "Number two, pull your head out of your butt, Marcos. And three, learn how to fricking spell!"

I wrote down some items I could work on, but the negative voice in my head was an all too familiar critical one. *Should I just work on the items that John detailed—or were his complaints symptoms of my deeper flaws that would require their own action plan?*

I sat and looked at the words on the half-filled screen. What I was hearing was an old voice from my childhood, a voice that always shamed me into shape for what others wanted of me. Echoes of "get your act together, apply yourself, what were you thinking, you can do better, Marcos" rang in my ears—the ghosts of an ADHD past, always within earshot, ever ready to pick my

9

bones clean again. I thought I had banished them when I got my undergraduate degree, which at the time seemed like validation that I *had* gotten my act together, *had* applied myself, and *had* done better. But they always came rushing back in to fill my lowest moments.

"You're beating yourself up," I whispered to myself as I thought about meditating to calm down and get back to the task. I opened my journal to the notes I had taken down that morning. *How many Ls in* professionalism*?* I thought as I studied the jumble of panicked handwriting.

"Damn it, Marcos," I muttered in disgust as I closed the journal. I could feel my critical mind closing in and I didn't want to be alone with those haunting thoughts. I needed to get up and get away. I needed a walk in the trees with Elliott.

Elliott had library duty at the school on Mondays and I hoped he would be able to leave early as I texted him from the parking lot outside.

"You're off work already?" Elliott asked as he approached the open passenger door dressed in skinny black jeans, a gray jacket covered in his handmade art patches, and his usual combat boots.

"Sort of," I hedged. "They gave me some time off to focus on a work project, but I feel like going for a hike. Wanna come along?"

"Sure, they won't miss me. No one comes to the library."

"Hop in."

"Can we go to the trail by the road tunnel? The one where we found the bones last time?" Elliott's voice rose with excitement. "I am looking for an elk skull for an art project."

"Sure, that sounds perfect for me right now," I said, already feeling my anxiety decrease.

Elliott always had a thing about bones and anatomy, even as a kid. We used to build models of dinosaurs, horses, and then humans. And Elliott learned the name for every single bone, even the tiny ones that weren't labeled. I drove west from Denver up into the foothills of the Rockies and smiled as I recalled a favorite bone memory from years ago. We had just moved up to human skeletal models and he had memorized every bone in the body. One day when he caught a fingertip in a closing door, I heard the scream and raced in the room to hear, "I think I broke my phalange!" It was terrible, but I was actually proud of her—*him*—standing there as I corrected and mentally scolded myself.

It had been an effort to get the name and pronoun thing right with him at first, but I still found myself getting it wrong in my mind when recalling the childhood memories—*another item for the action plan.*

We parked the car, and Elliott took a pair of rubber gloves and a thick plastic bag that he kept in the trunk for picking bones out of lifeless carcasses. His favorite trail started just off the highway before it disappeared into a tunnel through a giant mountain.

"There must be a lot of animals that cross here," I said to him, but he was already up the trail searching for signs of large dead animals.

"Found one!" he shouted back to me after a few minutes. "I think they get hit by cars and then struggle to get away."

I walked up to find Elliott already examining white bones that protruded through wounds and fresh openings where scavengers had been at work. The smell of decay caused me to step back. "You can see the breaks across this scapula, and these vertebrae are wasted," he said in a tone that sounded almost clinical.

"The head is gone," he conceded. "Something probably carted it off."

"I'll look around for it," I offered, eager to distance myself.

"See the hips? She was a juvenile," Elliott said softly. "Damn."

I looked around at the fresh snow that covered the tops of the mountains as I breathed in the fresh air that made John Gorman's demands feel a thousand miles away. I returned to Elliott, and he handed me a second set of gloves and the bag as he carefully took only the bones he wanted.

I watched him as he examined the poor creature before making his deliberate selections—three neck bones below the absent skull and four ribs broken from their vertebrae anchors. I thought back to us working on anatomical models and studying each bone carefully before placing it in its proper spot. When I recall those earlier times, it's like those experiences and memories happened with someone else—someone I still miss but feel like I shouldn't. The dreams I had for that earlier person are the hardest things to let go of as a father—the drama of a first boyfriend, a white wedding dress, or holding a newborn grandchild. Now, I just felt off script as I continued to learn who Elliott was becoming.

I can still recognize parts of that person in the boy next to me, but those parts feel different—not better, not worse—just different. Perhaps Elliott should be at the top of my action plan.

"There. I'm finished," he said, directing me to close the bag. "I'm going to leave the rest for the raccoons. They need the calcium."

Our drive home was quiet. I imagined that Elliott was thinking about the life of the animal whose remnant bones he held, which he would ultimately repurpose into something new and beautiful. My mind kept coming back to John's list and my response. The whole thing seemed so cheap and meaningless compared to the pile of bones. The animal was here one minute and then *boom*—a pile of calcium for some raccoons.

CHAPTER 2

I walked into the office on that last day and everything just felt off. It was too quiet, and several other artists were standing up in their cubicles.

"Marcos," came a voice to my left.

It was Gorman, standing in the open office doorway. *No, no, no*, I thought. *Not me. I've been improving.*

"Please step into my office for a moment."

Walking down to his office felt like sliding down a long slope.

"Marcos, we gave this a month, but the other directors and I just don't feel like you have made the performance gains we discussed and agreed to in your plan."

"But I started spell-checking everything, and I can feel the difference in mental clarity after I lowered my medication."

"I'm sorry, Marcos. It just isn't enough of an improvement," he said, reaching for a package of documents at the edge of his desk. "I have a separation package here. Today is your last day with us."

I moved forward in my chair to object, but he ignored me and continued in what sounded like a well-rehearsed script. *What more do you want from me? Just ask me. I can take a class*, I said to myself.

"In it, you will find your final paycheck and severance check, a job resource kit that the HR team put together, and some help lines if you feel you need them. You will likely qualify for unemployment benefits if you wish to apply; details are in the packet. Your company-paid medical and dental coverage will continue for another thirty days. We took the liberty to place some boxes outside of your cubicle to pack your personal belongings. Do you have any questions?"

Yes, is this all that ten years of effort earns me? I thought to myself.

"Please let me know if you need any assistance to pack up your things this morning," he said, standing up to open his office door.

I exited his office and walked over to my cube like a man freshly condemned. The only people who made eye contact were other older artists who were already packing boxes with their design awards and personal items. *If I still worked here, I wouldn't want to look at me either.*

I placed the packet on my cluttered desk and started taking my drawings out and laying them in the first open box. I looked at the pictures of Lilly and Elliott sitting on what would soon be someone else's desk. *What would I tell them? Would they see me as a failure?* I grabbed their photographs and set them on the top of my files just as Austin, the young artist in the cube next to me, poked his head around the divider. "Marcos, I'm sorry, man," he whispered. "I really enjoyed working with you."

I looked up from my grim task, eager to see a friendly face. "I enjoyed working with you too. That Sturdy-Mix portfolio you did was awesome."

"Thanks. Hey, all of us are getting together at Django's later for happy hour," Austin said and then nervously corrected, "I mean, it's not happy, but it would be good to meet up with you and the others after a tough day."

I smiled. *Tough day is right*, I thought, *and how many like it might follow?* The last thing I felt like doing was wallowing and commiserating over drinks, but I should be thinking about networking and building a list of people who might be a reference or introduce me to a new firm or creative director. "Sure. Let everyone know that I will be there."

I finished packing my professional life into just two boxes. I looked up at the gray December sky as I walked out. Light snow had started to fall on the windshield of the car.

I had never been a regular at the Friday after-work get-togethers and I felt even more of an outsider after being fired from the team.

"Marcos!" Daniel shouted over to me to join their table in the middle of the busy bar. Deb, Jerry, Amy, and Thomas, all fired too, sat with the artists who had just finished their day. "I'm so sorry, Marcos," came the first condolence. "I don't know what they are thinking, letting you guys go," came a second more general offering.

"Them's the breaks," Deb said over a frozen margarita. She tried to be flippant, but she looked like she had just been crying. "We're calling this one the *un*happy hour."

"I mean, your contribution on the Salsa Sisters account was epic. No way that we'd get to that dance step breakthrough without your idea," Greg said to me.

"That was a fun one," I answered.

"Oh, and the Tahitian Black Pearl campaign was brilliant," Amy offered in my direction. "'Diamonds are a girl's best friend . . . now meet her lover!' That was amazing."

"I'm going to miss working with you guys," I said as I looked at their solemn faces—*unhappy hour indeed.*

"I'm going to miss working altogether," Jerry replied.

"Are you retiring?" Austin asked.

"Most likely," the older man answered. "I've been at this for a while and the technology is turning it into a young person's game."

"But your freehand work is the best, Jerry."

"I'll do contract work if you hear of any, so keep me in mind."

"Keep me in mind too," I chimed in. "I really can't be without a job very long. I just bought a new car last year and all of a sudden, those payments look daunting."

"Oh, you'll get snapped up next week," Greg said as he clapped a hand on my shoulder. "You'll see."

"I wouldn't be so sure," Deb said, raising a hand to ask for a refill. "It's hard out there for graphic artists over forty."

"I don't think that's true," Austin said.

I knew that it was. After the initial performance discussion, I started noticing all the new faces—Gorman hadn't hired anyone over thirty since taking over.

"Middle-aged designers who don't make it to senior art director are like dinosaurs—on their way to a nicely illustrated fossil record," Jerry added.

I swallowed hard on my drink. *Maybe they were right. Maybe I should have been on the art director side of the business by fifty instead of still holding pencils.* But the thought of the extra stress and the politics never seemed like a good fit.

"I heard that Denver Designs is hiring," Austin offered.

"For interns," Deb corrected. "I just checked with my friend who does their storyboards."

"I'm a little past my intern phase," I joked.

"Well, Marcos, if you don't catch on anywhere, you could always use your new red Mazda to drive for Uber to make the payments," Jerry said as he clinked my glass. "Here's to the dinosaurs."

I felt completely deflated as I carried my boxes into the house. Elliott and Lilly were in the living room and they both immediately recognized that something was off.

"Well, I got canned," I said as I dropped the boxes to the floor and flopped onto the couch between them.

"Canned? Like fired?" Elliott asked.

I let out a long sigh as the humiliation rushed out of me. "Yes, fired."

"Why, did you do something wrong?" Lilly asked with a side-eye look. "Did you tell off that jerk boss?"

"I wanted to," I said with a smile as I envisioned my little girl letting him have it. "In the end, I guess I didn't do enough things right."

"That's dumb. You've been there forever," Elliott said.

It was true. I had been working there for most of their lives. It was the only job they had ever seen me have.

"Dad, you're an awesome artist," Lilly said as she laid her head on my slouched shoulder.

"I'll put the kettle on," Elliott said as he got up. "I'll make us all some tea. You'll get hired at the first place you try for. I know it."

I hugged my daughter and stroked her long brown hair while Elliott set up the cups. "They gave me a severance package. It's an extra two months' salary in a final payment. It's like a reward for working there for so long. It should be enough money for us until I find another job, but we can't be buying anything we don't absolutely need." I reached down and stroked the head of our pug as Elliott brought in the tea. My heart was so tender at that moment and their compassion and support soothed me. I turned the conversation to their days and Lilly cracked me up with pictures she had taken with her friend Eva as they worked on cosplay costumes.

After a simple spaghetti dinner, I took the boxes down to the basement and added them to the clutter. I started unpacking the first box by taking out the family photographs. Clearing a space on my desk, I placed the old photograph of Lilly to the left of the monitor and the new one of Elliott on the right side. I retrieved an older photograph of both of them in Sunday dresses at their grandparents' and looked at it for a moment before placing it facedown in the bottom drawer.

I sat in my worn office chair and took in the silence as I tried to settle my chaotic thoughts. *What should I do next? How long can I make the small severance check last?*

I drew in a deep breath and tried to start meditating to control the shock that was quickly moving through worry on its way toward panic. *Breathe in.* Put a resume together. My last resume would have been from 2002. *Breathe out.* Deposit both checks.

19

Set up a budget. *Breathe in.* Send out resumes and build an online portfolio. *Breathe out.* You can do this. One step at a time.

By that next Monday, I had compiled a list of activities I was confident would land me a new graphic design job in the next thirty days, two months at the longest. The severance package would last that long if nothing came up. I knew I would have to start paying for medical insurance after the first month, so I set a goal to try to get hired within four weeks to avoid any lapse.

An updated resume was my first item. I couldn't even get the ten-year-old file to open on my laptop, so I started over by using the Colorado Office of Employment guide Gorman had provided in the help section of the separation package. I was proud of parts of the work I had done over the past decade and detailing those wins took some of the sting out of Friday's blow to my ego. I showed the finished resume to four of my former co-workers, but only one replied, and their advice was to do online image searches to find more examples of my work to add to the accompanying portfolio. By the one-week anniversary of my firing, I had sent my new resume to ten design and advertising firms.

The second week brought a new routine—the morning email scan for job application follow-ups. I checked my inbox first thing in the morning, every morning, eager to reply to a request for portfolios, telephone interviews, or office visits to meet creative directors. By the end of the second week, I had two requests to see my artwork—but nothing else. I found seven more positions posted, two of them junior, and I applied for them.

Weeks three and four came and went with new applications going out, but only two firms asking for artwork examples. Each morning, I would hang my hopes on the inbox only to see the familiar rejection format. "Thanks for applying for our senior graphic designer opening. While we thought your resume was strong, it doesn't quite fit our needs. Good luck in your search."

Week five delivered the dreaded health insurance search and paperwork I had hoped to avoid. I had visited my doctor right before the company's extended coverage ran out. He put me back on my full dose of antidepressants and wrote me a double-sized prescription that I could fill before my coverage lapsed. But as I sat at my computer, swimming through the confusing options for coverage and deductibles, I kept one eye on a dwindling bank balance.

The second month was the real deadline, I remembered telling myself as I expanded my search to the neighboring cities of Golden, Boulder, and even Colorado Springs for larger firms that I could drive to if hired. But each day it became harder and harder to check an inbox empty of any positive reply. I started meditating in the morning to recover from the daily disappointment. "It's going to be okay," I repeated as a mantra every day, but I had a harder and harder time believing it.

At the start of the third month, I reluctantly went to the central office for Colorado Unemployment and filed for benefits to help stretch our remaining money until the end of the next month. I showed them my resume and brought along a handful of my favorite creative works, but most of the guidance was "Can you do anything else? Or what other work have you done besides the artist thing?"

"I used to teach ballroom dance," I answered as the case worker kept his eyes locked on the screen as he scanned potential jobs for me.

"We don't get much call for that one, I'm afraid."

The unemployment money helped and the weekly walk of shame to check in on my job search progress was tolerable. *Lots of things were becoming tolerable.*

I attended job fairs and tried to warp my design background to meet the needs of corporate marketing, software sales, and even social media advertising.

The full-strength meds helped again, but they felt like soft brakes on a runaway truck that delivered new anxieties daily. Near the middle of the fourth month, lack of regular sleep had eclipsed all other problems. I would lay in bed at night and chart the upcoming bills against the last of the savings and the next unemployment check—there was no getting over the hurdle next month. We were officially out of money, with only the remaining available balances on the credit cards as the last reserve left for us.

I thought about having the kids stay with their mother full-time, but I felt Elliott needed a man in his life—even an unemployed one. I thought about asking my mom and dad for help, but their relationship with Elliott had been strained since his transition. They try to love him, but still hold on to who he was, and every visit is another painful step of letting go.

Lying awake in a nervous sweat, Jerry's words from the unhappy hour came back to me. "Marcos, you can always drive

22

that new red Mazda of yours for Uber to make those payments."
So I got out of bed at 2:00 a.m. and filled out the application and
background check on my phone. The next sleepless night, I snuck
out of the house and gave my first stranger a ride to the airport.
By the time I returned home to make coffee for us, I had earned
seventy-four dollars.

Night after night, I snuck out of my own house while the kids slept,
and each night out felt like an escape from the obvious shortcom-
ings that everyone could see in the daylight. Halfway through the
fifth month of job searching, I was tired of struggling, was desperate for some financial relief, and just felt frustrated on all fronts.
I felt broken in ways that I never imagined I could break.

Worst of all, I could see that my fruitless job searching and
what felt like a darkening depression closing in were affecting
my family. I also started rideshare driving during the day to earn
enough to fill a grocery cart with ever more generic food items as
the quality of our diet declined. We deferred once-standard family
activities like pizza night out, and events that Lilly wanted to do
with friends now felt like luxuries. In the spring, when the kids'
clothes started to look a bit short in the limbs, I took them both to
the thrift store.

All these events eventually led me to the turning point that
changed everything, and it was all triggered by my father. I'm sure
he thought he was helping, but for the past three months he had been
emailing me inspirational Bible verses. They would hit my inbox
on Mondays or sometimes on Thursdays after a Wednesday-night
Bible study. I usually ignored them, but sometimes they did give

23

me something to ponder as I thought about how to fill the day ahead of me. A few times they reminded me of when my distant faith held a more prominent place in my mind—before I began walking down other paths. The passage he sent on that defining morning was Isaiah 41:13: "For I am the LORD your God who takes hold of your right hand and says to you, Do not fear—I will help you."

I sat at my desk and reread the verse. I had been up since 3:00 a.m. and had already been to the airport and back with passengers twice before taking the kids to school. *I could use God's help right about now*, I thought as I nursed the last of the morning coffee. *What the hell, God? I could use help from anyone's hand right about now.*

I fumed as I wondered what my dad was doing that morning as I was reading his email. He could be helping in more direct ways than this. Taking my kids out for the day would be a help—and offering to take both kids, not just Lilly. Removing older family photographs that made Elliott uncomfortable would help. Just trying to present gender-neutral holiday gifts to my son would help. I could feel myself getting angrier as I imagined him simplifying my current challenges down into a single Bible verse about taking a divine hand. I spent every morning in this inbox, looking for something to hold on to—something like a job offer, or even an interview, and the only thing I was being offered was Isaiah's quote about God's hand?

"Well, where's the hand, God?" I said out loud. "Where's the damn hand? Can't you see me down here in this damn basement, alone?"

My voice cracked with emotion as I spat out the accusing words. "I just don't know what to do."

I walked over and flopped on the spare single bed in the corner before taking in a few deep breaths to keep my negative thoughts from spinning out of control. "Even if you can't give me a hand, maybe you can just spare a finger," I murmured in a sigh. "Just one finger pointing at what to do next."

I remained silent and slowed my breathing until my mind started to calm down. After a few moments, I felt a soothing calm come over me that brought a serene silence that made me feel like I was somewhere else, in the presence of something else.

And then the words just came, clear and plain, like another voice in the room with me: "Just do the next good thing."

I lay there on the bed with my eyes still closed. *I heard that, I thought as I tried to stay in that blissful moment. For sure, I heard that.*

I started coming out of whatever that welcome serenity had been as I replayed the words in my head. *Was that a message to me?* I thought as I closed my eyes again and tried to get back to that quiet space to hear the rest of the message, but the feeling was gone, the voice was gone. I replayed the voice in my head as it felt like I was returning to normal on the bed. The words sounded so confident, so sure. *But was that the whole message?*

I felt the familiar doubts begin to creep back into my questioning mind. *What good thing? Will it lead me to a job? Was the voice talking about my son? Was it talking about everything or just the next thing? Where was the explanation to that simple guidance?*

I repeated the comforting words. *Were they a test, a leap of faith?* I lay on the bed for a long time as I processed what had just happened to me and I resolved to look for that next good thing in my life, whatever it might be. As I spent the morning searching for volunteer opportunities that all seemed like good things, I felt something rise in me that I hadn't felt in a long time—anticipation. I found myself looking forward to the events of the day in anticipation of finding that next good thing. And I hoped that I could find the resolution to do that thing. Besides, anything looked better than the trajectory I had been on.

CHAPTER 3

I started the laptop, closed my eyes, and drew in a few deep breaths to quell the anxiety that always rose with the morning job search. The familiar stress felt like fingers around my neck as the computer blinked to life. I let out a slow breath as I imagined opening the inbox and seeing an email reply from an enthusiastic HR director from one of yesterday's job postings. *Let today be the day,* I thought as I visualized the opening line of their response. "Hello, Marcos, thank you so much for reaching out to us. We would be very interested in speaking to you. Can you send us the latest portfolio of your work?"

It was a familiar routine, and I took a careful measure of the small reserve of hope that I could still draw from to keep it going. *How many more mornings like this will it take?* I opened my eyes to the brightness of the screen and saw the notification bubble hovering over the email icon. I felt a quick rush of anticipation as I thought about the promise that could be a click away.

I tilted my head back and raised my eyes to face the basement ceiling that had so often been the focus of prayers and meditations. That spot had once been a firmament, occupied by a well-known and steadfast God, but which was now an open place where vacancy cleared space for new voices. "Today, please let it be today," I whispered as I clicked to open the email.

Help Our Friend Joe stood at the top in bold as the only new message. It was a follow-up to one of my emails about volunteering.

> *Hello, Marcos, thank you for your interest in helping our neighbor, Joe Sabah. Joe is eighty-seven and a twelve-year survivor of a stroke that makes it hard for him to get around. Joe needs help about six hours each day from 10:00 a.m. to 4:00 p.m., sometimes longer, sometimes shorter. It involves light caregiving and housekeeping, assisting him on his computer and phone, and driving him to Perkins—he buys! We are looking for weekday help, and it pays $10 an hour. Marcos, if you would like to meet Joe and interview, he has time most afternoons after 2:00 p.m. Email me back to make an appointment. Thanks, Patrick (for Joe).*

I reread the email a second time. *Ten dollars an hour?* I thought. *Is that all I'm worth?* I leaned back in the chair, half in disappointment—half to make it easier to turn my face upward for help again. *Ten dollars an hour will not cut it. Ten dollars an hour is not even close to cutting it.* I closed my eyes again and took in meditating breaths to get back to that calm state that had felt so clear and comforting the day before. "Just do the next good thing," I whispered as an incantation, but the words just seemed to hang thin in the air without the conviction of yesterday.

I clicked REPLY but could not get past the first line of the response before stopping. *Do I really want to do this?* I thought as my hands hovered over the keyboard. *Am I really in a position to help anyone else when I need so much help myself?* I closed my eyes again and envisioned the day ahead. It was Wednesday.

Wednesday was unemployment day, when I would step through the faintly familiar motions of getting ready to go to an office, but instead I would be going to the unemployment office to meet with Phil, my advisor. Pathologically positive Phil, who wore optimism like an empowering armor against the waves of the now unwanted. I could tolerate Phil, right up until the inevitable career change conversation that would always delicately use phrases like "something more appropriate," "considering the competition," and "pivot," but that always ended up sounding more like, "Are you sure you can still compete in the young person's world of advertising?"

I dressed and imagined walking into the dreary Denver municipal building, old enough to be dated but not old enough to be charming. I would walk to Phil's desk, being careful not to make eye contact with others, all the while grateful that no one else placed their indicting eyes on me. I saw myself with a new list of job postings in hand that would be my evidence to Phil that I was still "getting out there." It was my token of exchange with the state for another round of needed payment. *Would taking a ten-dollar-an-hour job helping this man, Joe, potentially forfeit or end the unemployment payments?* The thought snapped open my eyes to the waiting email response.

29

I read the email details a third time and then did the math in my head. *Six hours a day was $300 a week. $300 a week could be groceries and gas; it could be the co-pay on Elliott's medication; it could be next month's utility bill; it could be the cheerleader uniform for Lilly; it could be art supplies needed to update my portfolio.* And the job included a free lunch every day. *What would that save?* I thought as I summed it up: $50 a week, $200 a month. I put my hands back on the keyboard. *Had things gotten so tight that free lunches might make the difference?*

My imagined day felt like familiar drudgery. "Why not," I said aloud. "Just do the next good thing," I repeated to myself as I tried to channel the clarity from yesterday before completing the response and asking for an interview on Friday. "There, it's done."

"What's done?" Elliott asked as he walked down the stairs into the basement.

"Good morning. I was just applying for a job. Well, not a real job," I corrected. "It's more of a volunteer thing."

"It's Wednesday, are you going downtown today?"

"Yes, I am about to get ready."

"Can I come with you? I want to go to the art store with you again. I can wait in the car or in the lobby for you."

I recognized the enthusiasm in Elliott's request. "I can't afford to buy any more art supplies for a few weeks."

"That's okay. I just like looking around, you know. We'll do that starving artist thing."

I felt a smile come over me as I absorbed the small joy of my oldest wanting to hang out. "Sure, Elliott. Start getting ready. We can stop there for a while on the way back, but I have some driving to do this afternoon."

I dropped off the last rideshare and looked at my balance in the mobile app as I toggled my status to offline. It was enough for groceries and gas for the weekend until the next unemployment deposit arrived on Monday. I held the phone and flipped over to email. There was no reply to the last two resumes, but there was a response from Joe Sabah. "Hello, Marcos. Please come by at 2:00 p.m. on Friday for an interview."

I looked up from the email and scanned the unfamiliar neighborhood for where the nearest grocery store might be and then looked back down at Joe's email. "Just do it," came the guiding voice again in the stillness of the parked car. "You can always change your mind later."

I typed the response before I could give myself time to think and change my mind. "Sure, Joe, see you then." I hit send and leaned back in my chair.

"Thank you," I whispered back to the voice. "I will follow, but I am inclined to follow any voice other than my own at this point." I laughed. "Just help me hold it together today. Help me get through today without losing it and that will be a win," I said aloud and then sat silently in the car for a few minutes before starting the drive back home.

I put a vintage Carlos Gardel record on the turntable and began to prepare dinner. The lilting tango rhythms floated the short distance into the kitchen and started my feet sliding instinctively on the beige floor tiles as I stirred. The music brought back memories of holding my ex-wife Ursula and moving her thin body through the personal code of spins and strides at our wedding. Graceful Lilly stopped dramatically in the doorway to the kitchen and struck a flamboyant pose against the white cabinets, flipping her long hair back as an invitation for me to lead her. This was *our* code. I stirred the pot with a flourish and placed the spoon on the counter before stepping over to her in time with the music.

I lifted my arms into a dance frame and stepped into the center of our small kitchen.

Lilly laughed as she walked over and took my hand. "Okay, old man, you think you got moves."

"Let's lose those spaghetti arms," I directed as I moved her thin body into a dance embrace.

She wiggled them around like a Muppet and settled into a nice, sturdy frame. "Great! Now this is your dance space, this is my dance space . . ."

"Oh my god! You did not just Patrick Swayze me," she said, laughing at me.

"He was a national treasure! Now come on . . . ," I said, straightening. "There's no laughing in tango."

Her laughter simmered down to a smile. "No smiling either . . . ," I said, laughing.

I smiled and led out the first stride. "Step back with the right foot first. That's right," I encouraged. "And . . . we're dancing," I said as I moved her through the basic tango steps and brought her back to starting position.

"Do it again," she commanded. "I can do it better."

I was about to start again when Elliott walked through the arched entry into the kitchen. I could tell from the look on his face that he needed something. "What is it, Elliott?"

"I can't find my meds. I think I've lost them."

"Where did you look?" I asked, breaking the dance frame with Lilly.

"I looked everywhere," Elliott said with anxiety rising in his voice.

"Let's look together."

"Okay," Elliott said in relief.

I turned to Lilly. "Can you stir this so that it doesn't burn?"

I followed Elliott to his room, to the bathroom, and finally into the living room.

"You see now?" Elliott asked.

"When is the last time you saw them?" I asked, feeling my thin calm start to wear through.

"This morning. I had them this morning when I took one."

"And where was that?"

Elliott paused for a moment, and I could see that his mind was racing and that my questions weren't helping.

"Do you have any more at your mom's house?"

Elliott nodded.

I nodded with him as I knew what was in store for me. "Well, we can't both be off our meds at the same time," I said with a smile that won a laugh from Elliott. "Get your shoes on, I'll drive you over there."

33

I walked back into the kitchen and slipped my left arm around Lilly as I turned off the burner under the pot. "I have to go to your mother's house with Elliott. We'll eat when we get back."

"Two car rides with you in one day, sorry to make you do this," Elliott said as I pulled out of the driveway. "Have you ever had one rider get you twice in the same day?"

"I've never had the same person twice."

"Sorry, I hope you're not mad at me, Dad."

I stopped and thought for a moment before answering. "I'm not mad, Elliott. I am just tired, really tired."

Elliott was quiet for several minutes before speaking. "It's going to get better. I'm going to get my crap together, you'll see." Elliott said the words with a growing confidence that I had begun to notice over the past few weeks.

I drove and wondered whether that confidence came from the medication the new doctor had prescribed or if it came from some place deeper inside him and was just now starting to find its way out. "I know it'll get better for us. We just need to focus on what is in front of us and then take the next step. The next step for me is to do some work on my tired art portfolio, and the next step for you is to go into that house and get your meds," I said as I stopped in front of my ex-wife's new house.

I sat in the silence of the car and watched Elliott run inside. I took several deep breaths and tried to enjoy the stillness as I let my mind wander to the art I would try to create after we finally got through dinner. Elliott raced back out of the house in less than a minute, bottle in hand. "Got 'em," he said with pride as he closed the door.

"That was fast."

"She had them set aside for me. She said she keeps a backup stash too," Elliott said. "I don't think she trusts me with them."

"Maybe she is just more organized than we are. We'll get our acts together," I said, trying to bring Elliott back to that glimmer of confidence. "Now let's get back to that dinner."

I finished the dishes and walked down into the basement that served as a personal refuge in the evenings. Sitting at the desk, I opened the old leather portfolio and withdrew a handful of my best drawings and illustrations, placing them on the desktop in series.

I studied each of them for several minutes as if trying to recognize the calmer, more centered, and confident artist who had created them. He seemed so unfamiliar to me now. *Can I ever get back to the productive place that nurtured these works?* I thought before my mind wandered to someplace darker. *Does the artist who created these still exist?*

I felt like I could muster just enough energy for a simple illustration before collapsing into bed. Walking over to the shelf of jazz records that always summoned the artist in me, I thought about who I should call on. "This calls for some help from Miles Davis," I said as I dropped the needle and heard the first notes.

I reached into the back of the portfolio for a clean sheet and then searched the desk for a pencil that was just long enough to be sharpened again and put to use. I squinted tired eyes at the blank paper and searched for the promise hidden within it as I adjusted the pencil stub in my hand. "Show me some magic tonight,

35

Miles," I whispered aloud as I kept my eyes fixed on the white rectangle and set an out-of-practice hand into motion.

The first gray lines on the paper came in short hesitating strokes. I felt like quitting and finding a better night to start this again, but I pressed on. After thirty minutes, I began to feel faint sparks of confidence returning to my hand as the pencil lines lengthened and began to flow into one another in graceful arcs. After another uninterrupted hour, I could see some improvement and began to recognize my art on a page again.

While I focused on the movements of my strengthening right hand, I began to feel a calming isolation building in the quiet basement, as though the flourishing right hand were somehow directing its idle partner to stack protecting bricks into a mental rampart that both could retreat into again on nights ahead.

I embraced the energy of the moment and my atrophied artistic hand seemed to be finding a rhythm. I could see the face peering out of the page, wanting to be seen. I focused on the eyes and thought about what expression she would have, what thing she had just seen or felt or heard that I could capture there, but the sound of Elliott's boots descending the stairs into the basement broke the spell.

"Dad, I've lost my medication," said Elliott from the sixth step, too embarrassed to descend further.

I sat down the pencil and then turned to him. "What?"

"I put them in my bag . . . I know I did. I'm sorry."

I tried to process the familiar sentence in my head and then looked at my watch. "Elliott, that was two hours ago."

"I think I lost them again, Dad."

I felt like the floor was falling away from under me. "You what?" I asked, unable to hide my frustration.

"I know. I said I would be better. I've looked everywhere. I'm just stupid," he said hatefully.

This has to be a dream, I thought, but staring into Elliott's now panicked eyes let me know that I needed to deal with this, now. "Okay, let's retrace your steps. We'll find them."

Elliott turned and trudged back up the steps allowing me to turn and look back at the woman on the page one last time. She was almost complete. She looked pretty, but she had no expression to share with the world. She was a blank—lifeless as a golem crafted by some inferior hand. I placed my left hand on the paper and crumpled it into a ball as I grabbed my leather journal with my right hand and started to follow Elliott up the stairs.

37

We searched the same places as three hours before and I even searched some unconventional spots like the garage and the tool shed, partially in hopes of finding even the first bottle and avoiding a drive back across town to my ex-wife's house. The longer we searched the more anxious Elliott grew and I knew I would have to stop and make the drive again.

I pushed down on the anger and frustration rising inside as I slipped my shoes on and grabbed the car keys and the journal. Elliott moved to put his shoes on, but I stopped him. I knew that I needed to do this drive alone. And I intended to follow my ex-wife's example and keep track of the medication myself from now on.

"I'll be right back," I said to Elliott, trying to sound calm but he didn't respond.

I started the car and called Ursula to ask her to have some of the backup medication for Elliott ready in twenty minutes. I drove calmly to the first stop sign and then a second, but three blocks away from home a wave of emotion washed over me without warning, and I eased the car to a cautious stop.

"Oh my god, I am just trying to be a good dad," I shouted and slapped both hands against the steering wheel in anger. "Damn it, God. Why do you keep kicking my ass? Like, don't you have better things to do than just kick my ass all the time? Can I get a break? Just one break." Tears welled up in my eyes and spilled onto my cheeks as I saw the headlights behind, urging me forward. I started driving again as the feelings of frustration continued to pour out of me. "How about a pat on the head instead of a kick in the ass? Is that too much to ask?"

I fought back tears for the rest of the drive but added nothing more to my pleas. I pulled the car to a stop in front of Ursula's house and was startled to see a man lying on the ground next to the curb. I stopped the car so that the headlights illuminated the motionless figure. I honked the horn to alert my arrival, but also to see if the sound would stir the man to life. It did, and I stepped out of the car and approached him. He looked to be in his twenties and had clearly been passed out.

"What's up, man?" I shouted over to him.

The young man rolled over on his side and squinted against the harsh glare of the headlights. "Hello," he stammered, trying to focus his eyes and find the voice in the darkness.

"I said, what's up, man?" I said with more authority this time, still feeling protective of my ex-wife.

Ursula opened her door and motioned me to come over. "What's going on out here?"

"I think he's drunk. Do you have the meds?"

"Here," she offered. "I can give you two. One for tonight and one for in the morning, you will need to get the script refilled tomorrow. And you will need to get two bottles."

"Thank you," I replied.

"Do you want any money to help pay for it?"

I was shocked by the question, even though I did need her money to help pay for it—but instead I thought about which credit card I could use that was not overdue. "That's kind of you, but I've got it."

"What about him?" she asked, pointing to the confused figure awash in headlights.

"I'll sort him out. He looks harmless. Go back to bed, and thanks for helping out with this."

I pocketed the two small pills that would get my family through to tomorrow and then turned and walked back to the man in front of my car.

"You're back," he said, trying to get to his knees.

"Yes. So, do you live around here?"

He managed to get up onto one knee and steadied himself with a hand on the bumper of my car. "My life sucks," he spat in disgust. "I've had it!"

I looked down at him and recognized the feelings at his level. "Why does your life suck?"

"Ah, I'm you know," he said, trying to shield his eyes from the glare, "I've got ADD man. And anxiety attacks! You know anxiety, man?"

I felt my guard lower a bit. "Yes, I know anxiety, friend."

"And I have a learning disability, and like, you know, I'm on the spectrum." His eyes finally found mine. "Autistic, well borderline, but still," he slurred.

"What are you doing here?" I leaned in close enough to smell the alcohol on him and mentally added that to the man's list of preexisting conditions.

The young man sat back down and ignored the question, preferring his own. "Why is life so hard?"

The question hit me like a punch, and I stared at the swaying figure for several seconds. "Dude, I don't know." My words seemed to fade in the night around us. "I just know that it is hard."

The man snapped his head up to face me with a newfound focus. "And nobody pets me on the head anymore."

I smiled and chuckled at his strange statement at the end of a strange night, "Yeah, I get it."

"Would you pet me on the head, man?" he asked sincerely.

I froze in shock at the question and immediately resisted, but then I heard it in my head again, as clear as a shout: *Just do the next good thing.*

"Yes, I will," I answered as some unseen force directed me to overcome my hesitancy as I sat beside him on the curb and began stroking the hair on the back of the young man's head. It felt like an out-of-body experience as my heart instantly filled with compassion for this stranger. But I chuckled to myself at how I would explain the scene if Ursula came back out.

The young man smiled and tilted his head into the motions as I continued petting him in a rhythm that seemed to calm him. "I think I'm ready to go home now," he said, looking up at me. "Will you take me home?"

Tears welled up again in my eyes all over again as I realized that *I* was the one now delivering the pat on the head I had asked for not thirty minutes earlier. "Sure, I'll give you a ride," I said, sniffling.

"That's great, man."

"What is your name?" I asked.

"My name is Jason," he said, starting to cry himself.

"Do you know where you live, Jason?"

He nodded.

"Can you show me the way?"

He nodded again. "Why are we crying?" Jason asked, confused, as if he had missed something.

I laughed and wiped at the tears in my eyes. "Sometimes we just get a break, like a ride home. Get in, Jason."

On Friday, I drove to the interview with Joe and pulled into the parking lot of a five-story white apartment building that looked like it could use a fresh coat of white paint. I instinctively grabbed my journal in case I had to take notes or instructions. Entering the small foyer of the building, I looked for Joe Sabah on the list of call buttons on the wall. I pressed the black button next to his name and waited but heard nothing. I looked down at my watch and was exactly on time. I pressed the button again and then stepped to the side to make room for a woman on her way out.

"Some of those buttons don't work very well. Who are you here to see?"

"Joe Sabah," I replied.

The middle-aged woman stopped in place and gave me a warm smile. "That's wonderful. We love Joe. Are you a friend, a client, or a new caregiver?"

I hesitated as I thought about my answer. "A new caregiver, I think."

"He lives on the fifth floor. Apartment 505. Go on in," she said, holding the door open for me. "The elevator is on the left."

"Thanks," I said, stepping inside.

The old brown elevator doors opened on the fifth floor, and I stepped out to see a short, elderly, balding man holding a younger man's supporting hand as they walked together down the hallway. I watched them take short, synchronized steps, and wondered if that was Joe. "Are you Joe?" I asked in a voice loud enough to carry down the hall.

Both men stopped and slowly turned. "Yes," the old man answered.

"Hi, I am Marcos Perez."

"Yes, how may we help you?" Joe asked in a welcoming voice.

I felt a flash of panic that I might have written down the wrong day for the interview. "I'm here to—" I stuttered. "I thought we had an interview scheduled. Home care assistance. Help our friend Joe?" I offered.

Joe looked up at the man beside him. "I must have forgotten to write it down. Let's go meet him." Both men turned slowly and cautiously started walking toward me. "Wow, did I mess that up? Hello, Marcos." He continued speaking as they approached. "I must have forgotten to enter that into my calendar. I certainly remember your name. Marcos! It sounds so dramatic. I bet no one ever forgets your name once they hear it."

I watched as the four feet shuffled toward me in a slow rhythm. Joe's left arm was thin and atrophied and ended in a permanently clenched fist that tucked up tight next to his chest. He was short but looked even shorter due to being hunched over. His bulbous nose held up thick glasses that magnified his warm brown eyes.

"Marcos, this is Patrick. He is one of the people who help me."

Patrick reached out his free hand to me as they approached. "Nice to meet you, Marcos."

I shook his hand. He looked about forty years old and wore a T-shirt, shorts, and flip-flops.

"Thanks for coming, Marcos," Joe said as he eventually came to a stable stop in front of me. "I would like to start the interview now if that is okay with you?"

I looked at Patrick for guidance and then looked down at Joe. "All right."

"Take my hand," Joe ordered as he let go of Patrick's hand and reached out to take mine. "Good," Joe said, gripping my hand with surprising strength. "Now, walk with me."

I swallowed hard and put my hand into Joe's.

"Place it under mine so that I can lean into it a bit," he said in a voice comfortable with giving instruction. "That's it. Perfect,

Marcos. Wow, first attempt." He turned to Patrick. "Go and open the apartment for us, will you? Marcos will walk me back."

I felt a knot form and tighten in my stomach as Joe turned back to him.

"Let's go, Marcos," Joe directed.

I took a deep breath and tried to gauge how long the walk would be to Joe's apartment door by how far Patrick walked ahead of us down the hallway. I paid attention to the weight and resistance I felt from Joe as I took the first half-step forward. Joe followed without issue, and I took another step, and another.

"Hey, you are pretty good at this," Joe said, stepping ahead at what I assumed was full speed for him.

I smiled in a pensive grin that betrayed the worry I felt at leading this man down the hall. And then it clicked: *I was leading him. I was leading, like in a dance.* I flashed back to teaching ballroom dance where I had stepped as a pair for years with old and young, slim and heavy, graceful and clumsy. And in each new embrace I had learned a new partner's ability in the first few steps, just as I was doing now with Joe.

"Have you done this before?"

"I have never been a care provider before, but I used to be a dance instructor, and this feels like that to me."

"Wow! That's exciting. What kind of dance, Marcos?"

I had Joe's rhythm now and it felt like we were walking comfortably as one. "Salsa and swing mostly. But I instructed tango as well."

"Wow! Patrick, did you hear that? Marcos is a dance teacher," he said as Patrick held open the door to the apartment.

"There could be some tango moves in my future. No dips for me, Mr. Marcos. Let's head over to the couch please."

The well-worn red carpet of the hallway gave way to a short gold and beige one from the '80s as we entered Joe's apartment. We stepped through a clean kitchen into his living room that featured a simple white computer desk and chair against one wall and an older brown sofa and reclining chair on the other.

Patrick closed the door and came over to assist Joe onto the couch. "Marcos, do you have any previous experience as a home care provider?" he asked as he sat in the faded chair opposite Joe on the couch.

I shook my head. "No, I've never done anything like this. From the posting, it looked like someone without experience could do it."

Patrick nodded and continued. "Do you have a car?"

I thought about the red Mazda that I had been so proud of six months ago and which now seemed like a folly. "Yes, I have a nearly new car."

Joe looked over at Patrick with the smile of a boy, "Nearly new, that sounds nice."

"Do you have a driver's license and insurance?" Patrick asked.

"I do."

"Good, part of this job is to drive Joe to appointments and meetings."

"And we go for lunch every day," Joe interrupted in a cheerful but thinning voice. "Do you like Perkins?"

"Yeah, it's the pie place, right?" I offered.

Joe smiled. "I had a good feeling about you, Marcos."

I couldn't help but return his infectious smile as I looked into his shining brown eyes.

"Joe, do you want to ask your question?" Patrick prompted.

Joe sat up straighter on the couch and looked directly at Marcos. "Why are you here?"

This was a question that I was not prepared for. "Well, I don't have a full-time job in my industry right now, and I"—I hesitated as I hunted for an answer—"I could use a little extra money and I think I can help."

Joe sat quietly and seemed unsatisfied with the answer. He studied me for a few unnerving seconds before leaning closer. "Why are you *here*?" he asked, this time with more emphasis on the last word as if trying to get to some deeper answer.

I looked into his eyes again and I let my mind race through the events that had led me to this couch in a strange man's apartment to interview for an underpaid job that I wasn't qualified for. I felt myself soften under Joe's gaze and the weight of reliving the past six months that had led to only a cryptic instruction from an unknown guide. A wave rose in me as I focused my watering eyes on Joe and began, "Well, I am a divorced, single dad. I lost my job last year and I can't find another one. I am broke and can't support my family, and ten months ago my son tried to—" I couldn't bring myself to say the words out loud.

I felt like I was floating downriver on a flood of pent-up emotion as I tried to keep my watering eyes on Joe, but I knew I could not stop now, even if it blew the interview. "I feel like my life is spinning out of control and the only thing that helps is to meditate and ask for guidance. And when I asked for guidance, the message

I received was 'just do the next good thing.' I did the next good thing two nights ago by patting a drunk guy on the head and then giving him a ride home."

I paused to collect myself before continuing. "And today I am here. I am here to do the next good thing, Joe."

I took a deep breath that calmed the welling emotion, "Sorry, I hope that makes sense," I concluded.

Joe sat quietly and studied my face for a few seconds before reaching out his good right hand to pat me on the shoulder. He then turned to Patrick and they both burst out laughing.

"He's perfect," Patrick said, catching his breath.

Joe turned back to me and offered his hand. "Take my hand, Marcos. You're perfect," he said in a comforting voice. "You will fit in here perfectly. You have the job. Be here at ten a.m. on Monday."

I was stunned and confused by their laughter but shook it off. I took Joe's outstretched hand and tried to smile along with them as they laughed and welcomed me. And then I instantly flashed back to the emailed Bible passage from my father that had angered me. *I will take hold of your hand and say to you do not fear; I will help you.* I held onto Joe's hand for a few warm seconds as if trying to recognize and embrace a message there. "Perfect. I'll see you on Monday."

CHAPTER 4

I felt a jolt of apprehension as the elevator slowed to a stop on the fifth floor. Walking down the hallway leading to Joe's, I tried to prepare myself for my new role as a caregiver. *What tasks might the work require? Did I know what I was getting myself into? Did Joe?*

His door was open a crack, so I popped my head in. "Hello, anyone home?" I asked.

"Marcos!" Joe answered. "Come on in. We left it open for you."

I stepped in and carefully closed the door behind me. Joe and Patrick were sitting in front of the computer in the living room.

"Good morning, Marcos," Joe said as he reached his good hand over to give mine a welcoming squeeze. "Are ya ready?" His clear eyes were bright and welcoming. He looked genuinely excited to see me.

"I'm ready to try."

"That's the spirit," Joe said. "You'll be a natural, and I can tell. Can't I, Patrick?"

Patrick smiled as he finished one last task and then reached over to grab a page off the printer. "This is the routine," Patrick said as he handed the two pages to me. "Let's start in the bathroom."

I followed Joe's caregiver down the hall to the small bathroom in front of what looked like Joe's bedroom.

I scanned the document as I walked behind him.

"Don't worry," Patrick said, motioning me in beside him. "Joe will tell you if you miss anything. He's not shy about things like that."

"Good to know."

"When you come at this time of the morning, Joe will have been up for a bit, and he will have had his shower. He usually hangs up his towel after he's done, but sometimes he misses. Marcos, you must keep the floors and countertops dry. Joe's eighty-seven and he had a stroke a few years back so we can't afford for him to have a fall. He uses a walker around the house but likes to use his special cane when going out."

Eighty-seven, stroke, no falls, no mistakes, got it, I said to myself.

"I usually just use that morning's towel to wipe everything down and then put it in the laundry bin in the bedroom before setting out a new one for tomorrow. Laundry day is Friday. The laundry is on the ground floor and Joe will give you the quarters to go down and do it for him."

Laundry, I can do laundry, I thought.

"Next is the trash. There's a can in here, one in the kitchen, and one in the bedroom. The one in the bedroom can sometimes have used Depends in it, so make sure you check it. Keep the shelf next to the bed stocked with new ones from the closet. The body starts to get a little wonky the closer we get to ninety years old."

Patrick must have noticed my reaction to the diaper comment.

"Don't worry. If he goes in the night, he does a good job at wrapping everything up. Now, let's move on to the pee bottles."

Pee bottles? I thought to myself before rejoining Patrick's instruction. "Okay."

"It's easy," Patrick said pointing to a clear plastic bottle with an oversized opening and flip top. "There's one by the nightstand. He uses pee bottles to relieve himself when he can't make it to the bathroom in time. The bottles are great really. It takes him a while to get up and make it to the bathroom and sometimes Joe would rather just *zip, zip, zip*, and get back to whatever he's doing. Just pick it up, dump it in the toilet and rinse it with some water."

Patrick picked up the pint-sized bottle and emptied it without a second thought. "I started using Lysol last year as a way to keep it clean."

Patrick handed me the cleaned bottle and nodded for me to put it back on the floor next to the bed. "You always have to put them back in the same place. Joe likes to know where his bottles are."

"There are more?" I asked.

"Yes, he keeps them at strategic locations around the apartment so that they are never more than a few steps away. Here, I'll show you."

Patrick walked me around the apartment and pointed out the same clear bottles on Joe's small computer desk, next to his recliner, and on a side shelf in the dining room.

So, this is what old age is like? I couldn't help thinking. *You struggle and suffer for decades and then your body just starts failing?* I looked over at Joe, whose watery, blinking eyes followed our every move as Patrick had me check each bottle before emptying

THE NEXT GOOD THING

two of them. *This was getting real for me.* Patrick and Joe seemed used to it, and I wondered how long it would be until I felt comfortable dealing with it, but I was getting used to lots of new things.

Patrick continued, "After the cleanup routine, I wash my hands and then start Joe's tea and his morning shake."

"Be sure to show him my favorite cup," Joe shouted into the kitchen.

"I'm going to miss that guy," Patrick said as he took a large red cup out of the cupboard. "Here, I'll show you how he likes it."

I memorized every detail from Patrick for the rest of the morning. Food preparation, shopping, doctors and pharmacies, emergency numbers and relatives, and every care detail down to when to change Joe's sheets. I took notes in my journal on every item until it was time to prepare Joe for his daily lunch.

"I warn you now, his favorite topic of conversation will be you. It's just how he is—so get used to talking about yourself."

"It seems like there is enough work to keep me busy," I said as I shuffled the notes on the kitchen counter.

"There is plenty to do for him, but he always finds ways to make it about you," Patrick said, getting a bit emotional. "It's his way, you'll see."

"It feels like it's getting close to lunch time, boys," Joe shouted from the living room couch. "Patrick, can you join us to show young Marcos my favorite booth?"

"Sure, Joe," Patrick said, wiping at his eyes. "I'd be happy to."

"So lunch is at Perkins, every day," Patrick said to me. "I'll cover that routine too. It all starts with getting him up and it ends with pinning the badge on him."

"The badge?" I asked.

"Joe, are you ready to go?" Patrick asked as he poked his head around the corner.

"You bet!" he answered enthusiastically.

"I'll walk Marcos through how to get you ready, Joe."

I followed Patrick back into the living room. Joe inched his delicate frame to the edge of the couch. He looked so small, so fragile that anything might be a danger to him. His eyes were brimming with anticipation as I approached him. *Did Joe already trust me to guide him safely?*

"Show him the chick magnet," Joe encouraged Patrick.

I looked over at Patrick, who just chuckled as he grabbed a walking cane crafted from gnarled wood. It was short to match his height, polished to show the streaks in the grain, and adorned with a large turquoise cap. "This is his walking stick. Joe prefers to use this when he goes out," he said turning toward his seated friend, "but the walker is much safer."

"Ladies appreciate a man with a walking stick," Joe answered while looking at me. "Now help me up, Marcos."

I looked over at Patrick for help, but he just handed me the cane.

"Offer your hand to him and keep it steady," Patrick finally said. "He will do most of the pulling to get on his feet."

Joe clamped onto my hand as soon as I reached out to him, and he got to his feet in one confident move.

"Take the cane in your other hand and walk me toward the front door," Joe ordered with a smile. "And no fancy dance moves."

"Just like you did on Friday, Marcos," Patrick instructed as he waited near the door.

I walked with Joe and felt that he was stronger than he looked. We paused near the door as Patrick fished through a small tray for Joe's apartment keys and white nametag. Patrick handed me the keys and started to put the pin on Joe's shirt.

"I want Marcos to do it," Joe said to Patrick.

Patrick handed me the pin. It looked like an authentic name tag from the restaurant and read THE MAYOR OF PERKINS. "Didn't one of your students have this made for you?" Patrick asked.

Joe shook his head as he waited to receive his medal. "The previous manager of the restaurant made it for me."

"Are you the mayor of Perkins?" I asked.

"Oh, you have no idea," Patrick laughed.

"So where do I put it?"

"It goes on the pocket," Joe directed.

I placed the magnetic name tag on the pocket of his polo shirt. "This looks like a real Perkins one."

"It is," Patrick replied.

"Now, we're ready to go," Joe said with contagious enthusiasm.

"Let me watch you walk him down to get into your car as the last step," Patrick said to me. "Then, you'll be on your way."

"But you're joining us, right?" Joe asked.

"I am, but I have to take off right after lunch so I will drive my own car," Patrick said as he closed the door behind us.

"Let's go see that nearly new red car of yours, Marcos," Joe said as he started walking toward the elevator.

I led Joe out of the building and wished I'd parked closer to the door as we walked together across the asphalt with Patrick watching from behind.

"Ooh, it's shiny," Joe said as we approached.

"Walk him to the passenger side and let him hold on to the door after you open it," Patrick directed. "Then take his hand and lower him into the seat sideways as if you were guiding him back onto the couch."

I followed Patrick's instructions, but each additional task felt like a new mission where failure was not an option. I needed to be on my game. *Was the ground under the door dry? Were there any stones he could slip on? Was the door in the right position? Were his shoes tied? Would every little thing be like a survival test as his home care provider?*

Joe lowered himself into the car seat and swung his legs inside. "The eagle has landed," Joe said as he took his cane and placed it between his legs.

"Nicely done," Patrick said.

My tensed shoulders must have slouched visibly as I closed the passenger door.

"Don't worry, it gets easier," Patrick said. "But I like the way you are careful with him. You'll do great, Marcos. I'll see you at the restaurant."

I nodded and let out a long sigh before walking around to my side.

"This is a very nice car, Marcos," Joe said as I got in. "Have you had it for long?"

"About a year," I said, thinking about the twelfth payment that would soon be due. I pulled out of the parking lot and followed Patrick.

"Do you like it?"

"I do," I confessed. "I worry now that maybe I should have gotten a used car last year. Do you remember on Friday, when I said that I lost my job? Well, the car now feels like a luxury—even though it's just a Mazda."

"These things have a way of working themselves out, Marcos. You'll see."

"I hope you're right," I answered. I really did like the car and was glad I had it now to help the man next to me.

"I am so lucky that you answered our email, Marcos," Joe said in a grateful tone. "It is such a blessing that people like you and Patrick come into my life. I couldn't do all the things I need to do without the help of people like you."

"You're welcome, Joe," I said as I reflected on what I was doing at that moment. *Is this what doing the next good thing looks like?* I thought as I wondered if I should be looking for some other work that paid more than ten dollars an hour. *Don't think—just do for a while. Look for the next good thing.* "We're both lucky that I was in a position to help out."

"We're here," Joe said as soon as the restaurant came into view. "Try to get us a place near the door if you can."

I pulled into the parking lot and found a spot under the green-and-white-striped restaurant awning. I went around to his side and checked the ground under the passenger door before pulling him up to his feet. He took my arm and led me toward the entrance with eager steps. We stepped carefully through glass double doors that led into a narrow entryway that ended at the pie counter before opening into the main restaurant. The manager looked up from the pie case and locked his eyes on us.

"Hello, Joe!" the manager said as he walked out to meet us. "What are you up to?"

"I'm counting my blessings," he said, squeezing my hand. "Steve, I want you to meet my new assistant, Marcos."

"Pleased to meet you," the manager said as he took my hand. "Thanks for taking care of our Joe."

"Well, it's my first day really."

The manager turned and motioned to a staffer to clear the first booth. "We're just cleaning up your usual booth, Joe. Give us a second."

The manager stepped over to the cash register to ring up a man who stood next to his two small daughters, both glowing in white dresses. Joe stepped with his cane toward the girls and bent over to their height. "And what are your names, little ones?"

"Lupita," said the older girl as she returned the old man's wide smile.

"Lupita is such a pretty name for a pretty girl." Joe turned to the younger girl, who tucked behind her father's protecting leg.

"That's Maggie," answered the father as he put his wallet back in his pocket. "She's a little shy."

Joe looked up and beamed a warm smile at the man. "She just feels safe with her daddy. You are so lucky that you have these two."

I watched the man's face fill with pride as he patted his youngest daughter on her head.

"We're ready for you," Steve said as he walked us over to what I gathered was Joe's regular booth.

The mostly older diners sat in green- and tan-colored booths, trimmed in pale wood. They all watched me as I lowered him into his seat.

"Hello, Joe!" came a greeting from a server as she walked by with two plates of food for another table.

"Hi, Betty. How is your mom doing? Better I hope," Joe said.

Patrick came in and sat beside me as two other servers stopped to talk to us. Joe knew each of their names and the names of each of their kids. He seemed to know details about what each of them was working on, struggling with, or dreaming about outside of Perkins. Benny, our server who immediately left a pot of coffee and cups, was taking night classes. Samantha was buying a condo. Alice was hoping her daughter would get a scholarship to Colorado State. Each of them came over from their other sections to chat with Joe and ask about me.

It was like a parade as retired people, apparently also Perkins regulars, one after another stopped by to speak with Joe. They all said their goodbyes to Patrick, and they all shook my hand and thanked me for working with Joe.

I was a bit taken aback as I tried to reconcile the image of Joe at home on his couch and this celebrity sitting across from me. "Is Joe famous or something?" I whispered to Patrick.

"I guess he is in a way," Patrick chuckled as he gestured for me to grab the bowl of coffee creamer cups near the wall. "You'll see, Joe just loves people."

Joe kept talking to an older couple about their grandchildren, but he pointed to his coffee cup and double-tapped the first two fingers on his right hand against the tabletop.

"I'm glad I came along to show you this," Patrick said as he shook hands and nodded to Joe's friends when they heard he was moving on. "Joe has a routine around his coffee. He likes his hot, so some of the experienced servers know to bring him a fresh cup or just leave the coffee pitcher as Benny does. He likes two creams, but only from the packaged creamer cups. The little double tap is a gentle reminder to me, and now you, to prepare his coffee for him so that he can keep speaking to his friends or his clients if he meets them here."

"His clients?"

"Yes, he mentors some folks and has some clients from his classes. He often meets them here and will want you to order for him and keep his coffee right."

"Classes?" I asked but was cut off by another woman who came to our table.

"Marcos, is it?" the old woman asked, extending her hand. "Thanks for taking care of our Joe."

I was floored by the activity and interaction everyone had with this old man. It felt like a sphere of happiness that affected everyone around him.

"Welcome, Marcos," Patrick said to me with a knowing smile as he clinked his coffee mug against mine. "You're in the special Joe club now."

I learned Joe's regular lunch order and what he liked on special occasions like today when he got to show off a new assistant. Patrick and Joe reminisced about their time together and it turned a bit sad near the end of the lunch when Patrick left for his appointment. I sat and finished every bite of food on my plate, then helped Joe box up the other half of his sandwich, which he said would be his dinner. Joe paid, as promised, and he seemed ready to leave after the lunch rush quieted down.

I got him in the car and then started to pull away when he reached over and patted my leg. "That sure was fun. Did you enjoy the lunch?"

"I did," I answered. "You sure are the popular one."

"Well, when you make investments in people it always pays a good dividend. Everyone sure liked you, Marcos."

"It seemed like they were sad to see Patrick go."

"Yes, I suppose so. But now they get the blessing of you, just like I do," Joe said, looking over at me. "Tell me about yourself, Marcos."

"Me?" I asked as I thought about what to tell him about myself. *Like the regular me—or the current me? The happy family man—or the man who now spends more time worrying about things going wrong than helping them to go right? The successful artist—or the guy who now empties another man's pee bottles?* "There's not much to say really."

"Oh, come on now," Joe started in. "We both know that's not the case. You told me quite a bit about your recent times in our interview on Friday. What about your work—what work do you normally do when you are not doing the next good thing, I think that's what you called it, by opening your heart to help an old man like me?"

"I'm a graphic artist."

"And what does a graphic artist do? Is it drawing and painting or is it more computer-based?"

I thought back to the online portfolio I had built that still seemed to be short of what the market wanted. "It's all those things. It's creating visual concepts that deliver a feeling or a message and then I produce the final art."

"So you create something that wasn't there, and you bring it out of nothing but your mind?" Joe asked. "Wow! Sounds like magic."

I looked over at him, but he kept his eyes straight ahead on where we were going. "Yes, the job is like magic sometimes," I said, paying attention to how much I missed the work right then. "But I think I'm slipping these days."

"Marcos, why would you say that about yourself?"

"Well, I was fired from my old job, and I have spent close to six months now hawking my wares to different firms and no one appears to like my work anymore. And besides," I said, thinking back to the unhappy hour farewell conversations, "graphic design is a young person's game."

"Baloney!" Joe interjected.

I looked over at him as his forceful objection caught me off guard.

"The older the better, I say. Older people have tools and resources that only come from being alive for a few extra decades."

"Well, I do have an extra decade under my belt." *Or two*, I thought as I remembered the young faces that kept coming through the door at my old firm.

"Are you passionate about graphic design work?"

His questions started to feel like a poke in the ribs, but when I looked over at him, he melted me with that wide grin and bright eyes behind his glasses. "I am passionate about the creativity. I like bringing new things into the world, but I struggle with the corporate parts of the work. Every piece of art or design has to tell a story or raise awareness or call to action—the art has its own little job to do for a company or a client or a brand. That takes time. For me, there needs to be time and space to dream and play with a concept before I can start nailing it down. But the business models and time demands can shortchange the creative process until my work starts to look like everyone else's. I don't feel like I perform my best under those constraints."

"Hmm," Joe said as though he was thinking about changing the subject. "Didn't you say you have a boy and a girl?"

"Yes, Elliott and Lilly," I said, reaching over to turn up the air conditioning in the car. "Elliott is a sophomore this year and Lilly will be starting high school. She tried out for cheerleading last week and she made it!"

"That's wonderful. You must be so proud."

"I didn't even know Lilly *liked* sports. I am proud of her, Joe." I could feel my face stretch into a happy grin. "She really wanted it, and she practices all the time. But I am worried about the uniforms though, they are crazy expensive. I had no idea."

"Don't worry about that stuff, Marcos," Joe said with a smile. "It all works out in the end. What about the boy?"

I noticed my smile fade away as I thought about him. My heart was heavy about Elliott. Some days he seemed like he was doing okay and then the next he seemed to start another downhill into a new dark area. I worried that he wasn't happy, but I wasn't sure there was much I could do about it. "Elliott is a great kid, but he is dealing with a lot right now," I said defensively.

"Do you want to talk about it?"

Wanting to talk about it felt like the problem I had been dealing with for over a year now. I *did* want to talk about it. I wanted to share what I was feeling, what I wondered Elliott must be feeling, how to let go of old memories and dream about new ones. But I didn't know if I could trust the octogenarian sitting beside me. All these experiences around Elliott were new but sharing them with older people hadn't won much understanding or tolerance. There was that word again—tolerance. *Why did I have to wonder if people would be tolerant of my son, couldn't I expect them to embrace him, or at least honor him?* I hoped that I was doing more embracing and less tolerating as I worked on being the father he needed. *What should that father do now?* I wondered as I drove us toward Joe's apartment. The next good thing would be to honor Elliott, at every opportunity.

"Elliott is transgender," I blurted out.

I looked over at Joe, but he just had the same happy look on his face as we drove.

"And it is a really tough road to navigate . . . ," I continued, leaving the sentence hanging, not exactly sure how to finish it.

Joe stared straight ahead for two blocks before speaking. "Well, that *is* a tough road. But Elliott will get through it. After all, he has a dad who loves him and is here to help him through the difficult parts."

I looked ahead as I replayed Joe's reassuring words and let them wash over me again and again.

"Elliott will get through it."

"He has a dad who loves him."

"Help him through the difficult parts."

I turned my face to the left toward the window to shield my emotion as I embraced those loving words. I couldn't explain it, but his reassuring words felt like a floor forming beneath me for the first time in ages. I had stopped falling. From this solid base, I could get to my knees and eventually to my feet again. I wiped my eyes to be able to see the road clearly.

"You're going to be great, Marcos," Joe said, reaching over with his right hand to pat me on the knee again. "You'll see."

I slipped out of the house after the kids were asleep to get a few more rideshare trips in. I set my goal at netting one hundred dollars. One hundred dollars a night for the next five nights would pay for Lilly's cheerleading uniform.

Each new pickup and drop-off took me a little farther from home and I kept wondering how Lilly and Elliott were doing at one in the morning. *Let's make this next ride the last one.*

I looked at the app and saw "Reuben 4.6 stars, pickup in downtown and drop-off in south Denver." "You're going my way, Reuben," I said as I tapped the Accept Rider icon.

I waited for him outside of a fancy bar next to the train station. "Reuben," I asked through the open window as a group of men emptied out of the bar.

"That's me, guys," a young man in a business suit said, turning around to shake hands and embrace the other four men in his group. "Great night after a great first day, gentlemen. Let's crush this tomorrow."

I confirmed his drop-off address and took off toward his home and then mine. "Are you celebrating tonight?"

"Yes, I just started a new job today. It's awesome. I took the guys out for dinner, and it turned into drinks and eventually closing the place."

"Congrats on the new job. What kind of work do you do?"

"Commercial real estate. This is a dream job for me," he said, slapping his leg in satisfaction.

Dream job, I thought as I drove on. *Must be nice.* "What makes it a dream job for you?"

"It's a combination of things, I think," Reuben began. "It just feels like a great fit culturally. This feels like the right thing for me to do, you know?"

"I think I know how you feel. I just started a new thing today too," I said, not sure if I should call home care for Joe a new job or a volunteer role that paid a little and offered a free lunch. "I just started as a home care provider for an older gentleman, but it doesn't pay enough. So that's why I drive for a few hours every night."

"How old is he?"

"He's eighty-seven and they told me he had a stroke a few years ago."

"Man, that must be rough."

I thought about his comment and wasn't sure if he thought that Joe had it rough, or I did for agreeing to care for him.

"My grandfather was like that in the end, you know, with a caregiver and everything. It was depressing. What's he like?"

I replayed his question in my mind for several seconds before I looked at Reuben in the rear-view mirror. "He doesn't seem eighty-seven. He struggles physically with some things, but he's sharp. And everyone seems to love him. He draws a crowd, that's for sure," I said with a laugh, but my words didn't seem to capture that air of positivity I had felt when I was with him. "He's happy. He's near the end of his life, he's half paralyzed, but he's really happy—like unsinkably happy."

CHAPTER 5

S itting in my car outside of Joe's apartment building on that second scheduled morning, I debated whether to go in or not. *This work really isn't for me,* I thought as I imagined taking care of Joe without Patrick for support. *Could I even do this on my own? Was working with this man just a way to hide from the career path I was falling away from or was it following the guidance I had asked for?* I had expected the next good thing to be a bit more approachable than pee bottles and soiled trash.

When I walked in, Joe immediately called out to me. "Marcos, Marcos, come here quick."

My heart raced as I closed the door and rushed into the living room, fearful I would find him in a twisted heap on the floor. But he was sitting in the black office chair in front of his computer looking at a YouTube video.

"Come and sit next to me, Marcos," Joe commanded. "I'm watching *America's Got Talent.* Go back to the beginning and hit play."

I pulled in a second folding chair and started watching the video with him as a little blond girl in a blue dress walked out onto the stage with a fluffy white rabbit ventriloquist dummy. She beamed with nervous anticipation as she spoke to the judges and introduced her rabbit friend, Petunia. "Listen to her song," Joe said.

We watched as the rabbit appeared to belt out "Summertime," while the small girl expertly sang without moving her lips. Four judges and thousands in the audience gasped in unison as her beautiful voice filled the auditorium.

"She's a ten-year-old who is following her dream of being a professional ventriloquist," Joe said.

I looked over at him as he watched. His eyes welled up with admiration for her determination, bravery, and ability as he drank in her performance.

"Wow!" he said once she finished her song. "She's proof that you can do whatever you want to in this world. Just look at her, Marcos. That is a person who found the song they came here to sing."

"You mean her song choice for the show?" I asked.

"No," Joe said, shaking his head. "Her passion, her dream of becoming an entertainer—it's her purpose in life. Each of us has one—I like to think of achieving your dream in life as finding the song we came here to sing."

I looked back at the girl in the video—her dream appeared to be coming true.

"She won the show, you know," Joe confirmed.

"So should I go get a ventriloquist dummy?" I joked.

"No, you should discover what your dream is—and then you should follow it," Joe said, reaching up to pause the video. "But we'll have plenty of time to cover that when you're ready. First, I would like you to make the bed and empty my bottles. And after that, I have a new job for you—I'm promoting you to be my business assistant!"

I finished the morning chores and made myself a cup of tea to go with his. Joe moved over and motioned for me to sit in the folding chair next to him in front of the computer. "Okay, you are driving," he said before sipping. "Are you an Apple guy or a PC guy?"

"Apple."

"I had a good feeling about you, Marcos," Joe said with a wry smile. "Patrick was a Windows guy and it took him a while to get the hang of my system."

System? I thought as I looked over at the man who should have retired twenty years ago. *What system?* "What do you need me to do, Joe?"

"Let's start with my subscribers. I like to check that once a week. It's like housekeeping. I made a system so it's easier for my assistants to help me. I can still do it, but it's just faster if I can guide you through it. See that purple icon in the center of the screen?" Joe asked with a pointing finger. "Click it. It opens FileMaker."

"You have subscribers?" I asked turning to look at him. "Subscribers to what?"

"To my course on how to become a paid public speaker."

My mind flashed back to lunch yesterday. "Patrick said you taught a class or something."

"Yes, you'll see soon enough," Joe said, pointing back to the screen. "Now click on the icon."

Following his direction, I opened the file. "Tell me about this course, Joe. Were you a public speaker?"

"Yes, but that was a long time ago. Now I just teach people how to do it," he said as he watched me navigate his applications. "Stop there on the contacts tab. Now go back to the home screen and look for the Loop mail icon. Click it."

I opened the unfamiliar email application and followed his verbal navigation.

"Open the unsubscribe tab," he commanded and then leaned in to read the names of three people who had unsubscribed. With a little disappointment in his voice, he read, "'Catherine O'Halloran'; really, Cathy?"

"Did you know her?"

"Sure, she took my class. I even mentored her for a while. She had a great story and a lot to share with the world," he said as he leaned back in his chair. "Well, some do, and some don't . . . some will, and some won't."

Joe pointed to the bottom of the screen. "You see that magnifying glass icon? Click that and then highlight her name. Copy and paste that—you know how to copy and paste, right?"

I smiled and laughed to myself. "Yes, Joe. I've got it."

"Now paste her name in the unsubscribed tab back in FileMaker."

I updated his spreadsheet with the other two names before curiosity caused me to mouse over the contacts column to highlight the total number in his list. I was stunned at the number in the lower right corner of the application—nearly fifteen thousand.

"Joe, there are a lot of names on this list," I blurted out.

"Well, I'm older than algebra, Marcos," he said with a wide grin. "I've been at this for a while. It adds up."

"What do you do with them?"

"This is my database. The people in there are my lifeline. I'd be on the breadline without them."

Turning my head back to the screen, I started scrolling through names as I looked at the contact information—most were from Colorado, but there must have been a few thousand from other states too. "I still don't understand, Joe. Do they donate to you or support you somehow?"

"No, Marcos. They're my students, my customers. Let me run you through it," Joe said, shifting positions to get comfortable with his tea. "Go back to the home screen and click on the calendar application."

Opening his calendar, I was surprised to see an appointment for today at Perkins. "Tanya Dolin," I said out loud.

"That's right. We're meeting her today for lunch. Go back to the database and search for her name."

A quick search showed that she had attended a class the year before.

"Tanya took my class, How to Speak for Fun and Profit, not too long ago. She signed up for a promotion that included four follow-up mentoring sessions. We're doing the second one today. You'll get to meet her. She's amazing."

I looked back over at the old man nestled into the brown recliner across from me as I tried to make sense of what I was seeing and hearing. "When is the last time you ran that class?"

"It's been about three months, I guess. It's about time to run another one. I usually ask my home care assistant to help me run my half-day class." Joe added in what amounted to a request.

Oh, I had to see this, I thought. *This* had *to be the next good thing.* "I'm in Joe, 100 percent. How do we start?"

"Great!" he said, brightening even more. "Go back to Loop mail and let's start a new special offer. 'Get a free lunch coaching session with Joe Sabah.' Right-click on templates to get started."

Over the next hour, I opened templates, made changes, selected names to send the offer to, and even snuck in some of my own creative design flair as he spoke command after command to me like a human Siri—click this, copy that, change the date, email to reserve the room again.

Step by step, I learned his entire system and found that his business was profitable, allowing him enough money to pay his living expenses *and* to pay what was now my paycheck. I discovered that he had written a book on how to become a public speaker and another on how to get your dream job and he used those to get interviewed on podcasts and radio stations. *Radio stations? Joe was on the radio?*

Joe blossomed as he showed me how he maintained contact with thousands of former students and readers of his book. He swelled with pride as he showed me how he had designed his course with details down to the color coding of handouts and assignment sheets—light blue pages for speaking tips, light green for tips on how to build speaking topics and test them, light yellow for how to find groups and organizations that hire speakers and those who let new students speak for free.

71

"You'll see how it all comes together," he beamed. "I can't wait to do the next class with you, Marcos."

I was amazed at what this near ninety-year-old stroke survivor was still able to do. At the end of a busy hour, I had learned it all and we had a new promotion ready to send for a class in two weeks. *Would I still be here in two weeks? Part of me hoped so now. Is this Joe's purpose? Is this the song* he *came here to sing?* I wondered as I saved our last changes.

"Okay Joe, all we need to do now is set the price for the hour-long coaching session," I said as I looked through his sent campaigns and saw past promotions for fifty or a hundred dollars.

"How about fifty dollars?" I asked, eager to continue this fun collaboration with him.

"You're a full-sized fella and I've seen you eat. Better make it seventy-five. Let me proof it quickly," Joe said, leaning over toward the monitor. "Make it a little bigger for me."

Joe squinted through his glasses as he read over the email and double checked the distribution list of the sixty targeted names. "It looks good. Hit send!" he declared before finishing the last of his tea. "You are doing great, Marcos. This is so much fun."

It was fun. "What's next?"

"It's getting close to lunchtime. We'd better prepare the content for the meeting with Tanya. Grab some of the pink paper and grab some yellow too. You'll need to print out some of the outreach and topic refinement scripts for her. And grab a radio and podcast outlet CD from the shelf."

Joe took a deep breath and smiled after I had readied the kit for Tanya. "Wow!" he shouted. "That's a lot of work. Good job, Mr. Marcos. Now get the parking pass and my mayor pin and let's go meet her."

We walked through the front doors together and I noticed a well-dressed woman with her hair pulled back sitting in Joe's booth. She looked a few years younger than me and wore a sharp business outfit as if she had just come from an important meeting. Joe's face lit up as he waved, and we headed over.

"Wow! Who is this fashionable woman sitting in my booth? I love your blazer!"

She sprung to her feet and leaned down to hug him. "Joseph Sabah, you are such a charmer. How *are* you?"

"I'm well, Tanya. Please meet my new assistant, Marcos."

I shook her hand and lowered Joe into the booth. I could tell they were genuinely excited to see each other.

They took a few minutes to catch up before Joe got to the point of the meeting. "Tanya, what would you like to talk about?"

"Well, after taking your course last year, I took your advice and signed up for Toastmasters. It was exactly what I needed, and I got some constructive feedback from the group. It was hard to hear, but it made me one hundred times better as a speaker and my confidence was off the charts going into the first talks."

"That's great, Tanya! I'm excited to hear that. What did you talk about?"

"You might remember from our first meeting that I love the financial world, investing, and real estate is my passion."

"That's right, I remember," Joe assured her before changing to a demanding tone with his next question. "So are you out speaking?"

Tanya looked down at her coffee and sighed. "Joe, don't be disappointed in me. I started strong. I used the system, got some free gigs just to build my confidence and skill, but I just lost my energy and momentum."

"You have to keep going," Joe insisted.

"I know, I know. Speakers speak," she said as though repeating a line she must have heard from Joe before. "I know I should have just lined up some more gigs and gotten out there, but I—"

"Tell me what happened. This topic is your passion, Tanya."

"I *am* as passionate as someone could get about investment strategies, but my feedback cards were not what I expected."

"Did you get some dingers?" Joe asked.

The professional-looking woman I had seen from the entrance doors now looked like a struggling student.

"I did, but what felt worse is that some people just didn't even bother to fill them out. I think I knew at the time that I was losing them by the glazed-over looks on their faces."

"Oh my dear," Joe said, reaching his hand over to her. "It's hard to put yourself out there and get back less than you had hoped for. Sometimes you can be off, but sometimes the audience can be off. That's why you have to *keep going*."

Joe let the last two emphasized words sink in before turning to me. "I think I have something that can jump-start your energy to get back out there. Marcos, can you hand me the green sheet we prepared for her?"

I passed it over the booth table to her as Joe double tapped two fingers on the table next to his empty coffee cup as my signal to set him up.

"Tanya, did we ever talk about finding your song?"

A puzzled look came over her face. "No, I think I would remember that."

"I've worked with a lot of people and a lot of really amazing speakers. All the great ones have one thing in common: passion for their topic," Joe said in a voice that sounded full of wisdom and experience.

Something about his tone made me quietly reach into my small backpack for my worn leather journal. I cracked it open and started writing as he continued to speak.

"Tanya, I believe every person is put on this earth with a passion to do something. For some it's teaching, for others it's working with alcoholics. I even had one woman who liked to show people the benefits of traditional Chinese acupuncture. Each of these people had one thing in common—they followed their passion for teaching, substance abuse, or sharp needles. They found their calling or what they were put on the earth to do. Those people would do that work whether anyone paid them or not, and it was that passion that fueled them enough to stand up in front of a group of complete strangers and talk about it."

Looking up from his words that were filling my journal page, I saw that Tanya was completely captured by what Joe was saying—as was I. The small Joe who held onto me when walking

75

and who needed me to make his bed and empty his relief bottles, now seemed like someone else, someone new and revitalized as his keen mind guided his student.

"I call this finding the song we came here to sing. Find *that* and you are on your way to a fulfilling and happy life where you will want to share it with others. Most of the time, that person's song has the ability to solve a problem or is related to some past pain that *you've* overcome and can help others do the same. When you find your song, the next thing to do is communicate it in a way that solves that problem or pain for other people, then find a way to sing it for others through public speaking."

Joe's voice strengthened as he continued. "So, Tanya, what song did *you* come here to sing?"

As I finished writing, I asked myself the same question. *What song did I come here to sing?* My mind sorted through the past year: *what was I passionate about? What would I enjoy doing whether or not someone paid me? Did I even have a song?* I questioned myself, but all the answers sounded off-key.

I looked up from my journal to see the stunned look on her face. Tanya seemed to be struggling with the question as well. I looked over at Joe, but he just sipped his coffee as he waited for her answer. I was glad she was the one expected to answer and not me.

"Let me help you," Joe said as he broke the lengthening silence at the table. "Tanya, you said you have a passion for finances. But what is it about people's money that makes you passionate? Have you seen others struggle with their financial situation? What is the compelling element?"

She sat and thought about his questions before she began. "People's relationship to money is the most interesting thing to me. Folks can suffer a great deal when it comes to money if they don't learn about it. I think most people would rather think about something else, anything else."

Joe tilted his head a bit to the right. "You said something interesting there, Tanya. You said *suffer*. That's interesting to me. Let's explore that. It's good, it's something we can work with. Tell me about that pain surrounding finances." Joe asked the question in a way that seemed directed at her personally and not at the other people she imagined as her audience.

"Well, I know about this pain from my own experience. I didn't grow up in a wealthy home. Far from it. There was a great deal of tension around money in my family and we suffered." Tanya paused and I could see the emotion on her face as she recalled a difficult memory from her youth. "You could feel the fear around money, it felt like scarcity. My mom was stuck in an unhappy marriage, my sister and I were stuck going to a crappy school, and my dad was stuck in a dead-end job. We were all stuck. And I vowed to get myself unstuck."

"And you did, Tanya," Joe said with a reassuring smile. "That is so great! I think you found the problem for your worksheet exercise. "People suffer and live in fear when they feel stuck and afraid about money."

"That's it exactly," Tanya said as she dug through her purse for a pen and started taking notes on the yellow worksheet I had handed her.

"So what is the solution?" Joe asked, leading her now.

"You don't have to be afraid of money! You are not stuck!" Her eyes lit up as she spoke and then stopped to capture some notes. "If people just understood that with some simple changes they could have freedom."

"Wow! Freedom, that is powerful," Joe encouraged. "The next step is: what action do you want your audience to take?"

I could see she was brimming with ideas now and I found myself taking my own notes as ideas brewed in my head.

"There is so much," Tanya started. "First thing is don't get overwhelmed and freak out. Think of small steps. Money isn't a problem you hide from—it's your life partner. You get good at that partnership and you are rewarded with freedom."

Joe leaned forward and jumped in on her building excitement. "Yes! I love it, Tanya. Write that down. Get your audience to partner with money and get rewarded with freedom."

She scribbled it down as he spoke. "I love this! Thank you, Joe."

Joe took a long sip from his cup as she wrote. "I think we have you jump-started on the message building worksheet that can sharpen your next talks, but I think *you* just stumbled onto something even more important."

She took a few seconds to finish her notes and then looked up, ready for more from her mentor.

"It's your song, Tanya," Joe stated. "You were once stuck and afraid, but now you are free."

"And I want to give this freedom that I have to others," Tanya affirmed with building confidence. "I can show them the way."

"That's right. This is the song you came here to sing," Joe declared. "Congratulations, Tanya, you've just found what you should be doing for the rest of your life."

"Do you think I can?" she asked as if seeking his permission.

"Well, I wouldn't want to stand in your way, Ms. Dolin," Joe laughed and looked up at me. "And you know you've found it because you won't just *want* to give your newfound freedom to others—you will *need* to, *have* to. That's the way the song works. It will drive you to work harder than you ever have. It will drive you to stand up in front of strangers to share this passion for how they can be free like you. Give *that* message to people and you won't get any glazed-over eyes. Wow, what a day!"

I could feel the emotion coming from both of them as they continued to work over the rest of the lunch. It was so positive, so energetic, and so catalyzing—I couldn't help but smile and just share the moment with them as I quietly wrote down some thoughts on how I could use what Joe was sharing with his student. As I wrote, I felt that same reassuring floor under my feet that I had felt in the car with Joe after I'd shared details about Elliott, but now I also felt a first step forming in front of me. *Keep doing this. Keep doing good things. Look for the next one*, I told myself as they wrapped up their lunch with a long hug and a promise of a follow-up meeting.

I took Joe back home and started the afternoon routine of check-ing emails, making a pot of herbal tea, and setting him up in his recliner.

"You were really amazing today with Tanya," I said as I poured his tea.

"Wow! Thank you, Marcos. That is a very nice thing to say," he said as he wriggled into the comfortable spot in his well-worn chair. "What amazed you?"

He seemed so normal now, so Joe again as we sat there in his apartment. "It was you. You were so great with her. I followed along. It was like you were bringing the right answers out of her, like you knew what was inside her all along."

"Well, that's what I do. I help other people discover their meaning in life so that they can share it with others. I couldn't stop doing it if I tried, Marcos."

I believed that. That drive had to be where he summoned the energy and wisdom I had seen over lunch that had transformed the old man in the chair before me. "Do you think she can do it?"

"Sure! You can do whatever you want to in this life, you can have whatever you want. You just have to help others get what *they* want. This is one of the lessons I've learned in a long life— you have to give before you get."

"Give before you get," I said out loud as I made a note to write that nugget down.

"Let's say you want something—like a good-paying job."

"Good guess, Joe," I said with a nervous laugh.

Joe chuckled and then got back to his point. "You try and try with all your might to get a good-paying job and what happens?"

All of a sudden, I felt like Tanya trapped in a Perkins booth as his question hit me personally. "Well, I can tell you that I didn't get a job."

"Exactly!" Joe said, catching me off guard. "So *then* what are you doing?"

"I don't know," I said, unsure of how to answer. "Not getting a job?"

"Well, focusing on the *getting* is one way of looking at it, but how's that working for you?" Joe prodded. "And do your kids see you 'not getting' with all your might, month after month?"

His words hit me like a slap. "What am I supposed to do, stop looking? Stop trying to get what we need?"

"This is a powerful lesson, Marcos," Joe continued in a serious tone. "Sure, you didn't get what you wanted—not yet anyway. But until then, maybe your focus should be on what you are *giving* to others until it is your time to *get*."

I stood there repeating his words in my mind, trying to make them fit into what my life felt like now.

"You still don't see it, do you? Marcos, you are helping me with my needs—like my dinner tonight," he said with a smile as he held up three fingers to direct me to bring him three Ensure drinks and three Almond Joy candy bars, his nightly dinner routine. "But you are also helping me with my business. You are helping me succeed, and the thing about success is that it is contagious."

Did I help him achieve his goals today? I thought as I placed the bottles and candy bars on the table beside him.

"We helped Tanya today. Her success is as sure as the sunrise," Joe declared enthusiastically. "It was exciting to see that today, wasn't it?"

It was, and I could feel myself pivot as I remembered how I felt in the booth with them, sharing that moment. *Would that have happened without me giving my time, my car, my guiding hand?*

"We helped Tanya together, Marcos. And we will help others like her who sit in front of us. Just think about all the people in the database who can use our help," he said, beaming with satisfaction. "This is how I have succeeded every day for all these years, despite my setbacks. You just have to give first to start that success and then live in it until you get it back. Keep giving, Marcos, and before long, your turn will be next."

He was right. I wasn't seeing it. The good I was doing was sitting in the booth across from us an hour ago. And today's good thing would be delivered to Tanya's audiences far into the future. I tried to feel myself as part of that success and I wanted to turn on the computer again to check Joe's calendar for his next mentoring session so that I could experience that once more.

Joe could tell I had gotten his message. He reached out to pat my hand and then grabbed it. "And if you want love, my boy, give that too," he said as he raised my hand and kissed it. "Great job today, Marcos. See you tomorrow."

Getting into the car after leaving Joe, I turned on the Uber app right away. I wanted to get extra money, but I hoped to be able to give a little of what I felt I had just received. Each rider I picked up listened to my story about seeing my old Joe transform into a powerful coach with a valuable lesson. And that night, like a magic trick, each new rider opened themselves up for advice on some challenge in their lives. One young woman wanted to know if she was nuts for not wanting to settle down with the woman she was dating. A man wanted advice on how to talk to his wife about his drinking. Another woman on her way to the airport thought she wasn't getting the consideration she deserved for a possible promotion.

"Have you asked your boss what he needs and then worked on giving that to him?"

CHAPTER 6

A few days later, Joe interrupted my morning routine by asking me to check his email and read any new messages for him. I made us both a cup of tea, then sat in his computer chair.

"The first one is from producer@krrf.com. It reads, 'Thank you Mr. Sabah for your inquiry to be on the *Mornings with Mike* show. While your suggested topics were interesting, we just don't think they are a fit for us at this time.'" I could have finished the rest of the email rejection from the fresh memories of receiving so many myself.

"Well, that's a miss. Next!" Joe said, interrupting me from reading to the predictable ending. "Go to the follow-up file and mark them for another email in six months. What's the next one?"

Joe let the rejection slip right off him. I looked over and he seemed energized at the opportunity to go through his inbox. *That's not been my experience lately*, I thought as I moved to the next message.

"It's from Sam Burrows. It reads, 'Joe, sorry for the delay in response. I am still working on the short article you asked me to write about my progress. Please give me a few more weeks to get that done. I hope you are well. Sam.'"

"Weeks?" Joe protested. "He's been working on that since February. Well, some do, and some don't. Marcos, type out this reply, please. 'Dear Sam, I look forward to seeing the write-up that you promised me earlier in the year. I know you can do it. You just need to set your mind to it and focus until the work is done. Sam, if we were together, I would sit with you until you completed the assignment. But you are not here, so I hope you will keep this email open on your computer as my watchful eye until you complete the task. Love, Joe.' Let's see if that's the thumb in the back that he needs to get going."

"Thumb in the back?" I asked. "I don't know that saying."

"It's one of my own," Joe said with pride. "I've been using it for decades with my students. When I put my arm around you to help you, I will either pat you on the head to praise you or lower my arm to jam my thumb into your back to motivate you to keep going. What's the next one?"

"It's from Tanya," I said and noted the enthusiasm in my voice at hearing a follow-up from that meeting.

"Read it!"

"Sure thing. 'Dear Joe, thank you so much for your wisdom and insights at our lunch last week. You will be happy to know that they worked—boy, did they work!' She even used an exclamation point there," I said as I looked over at Joe. He was beaming with joy as he sipped his tea.

I went back to the screen to continue reading. "'I went straight home and retooled my talk track, and more importantly, restarted my outreach to book new speaking engagements for my revised content. Joe, I feel like you really unleashed something inside of me. I have more energy now and I am just driven to get this message out to new people. I am so glad I took your course, and I am even more grateful that you offered your precious time to me. Thanks for helping me discover my passion. All the best and talk to you again soon, Tanya.'"

Joe sat for several seconds and seemed to be savoring her words and thinking about a reply. "Type this reply, Marcos. 'Tanya, it was my pleasure to help you. Call me anytime. Joe Sabah.' Please read that back to me once before we send it."

I read the email draft back to him and felt Tanya's excitement from the meeting wash over me again.

"That's good. Please hit send," Joe said. "Wow, we won a breakthrough with her, didn't we?"

"Yes, I was just thinking the same thing. You really helped find her passion, Joe. She seemed like a new person at the end."

"She is finally the person she is supposed to be," Joe corrected as he turned his warm eyes to me. "But, what about you, Marcos?"

"What about me?" I countered nervously as I started to feel the chair heating up underneath me.

"What is Marcos passionate about?" Joe started. "I wonder what Marcos's song will be."

His question started to feel like—a thumb in the back. The warm feelings that came with remembering Tanya spark to life in front of Joe quickly cooled as all I could think about for myself was the overwhelming fear of failing. The stress in my neck was so tight it felt like the life was being throttled out of me. "Well Joe, it's hard to think about my passion. I am kind of in survival mode."

"Survival mode," Joe repeated, his eyes filled with compassion. "There is a lot of fear in that statement, Marcos. Fear likes to come forward and take center stage. It's a real prima donna. If you let fear be the star in your life, everything else will have to revolve around it."

I thought about his statement and immediately knew he was right. I felt that truth every day. "I know, right? Everything just seems to swirl around my fear when I am anxious."

Joe perked up in his chair. "Stop! Do you see what you just did?"

"What?" I asked defensively.

"Marcos, you just said, 'I am anxious,'" Joe said, inching to the edge of his seat—ready to make his point.

"Yes, so—"

"Be careful with the words you use. The words we speak, especially the words we speak to ourselves, have deep meaning. So when you say 'I am anxious,' you are defining yourself. Words are powerful. You are not anxious—you are Marcos. *Be* Marcos, a wonderful and beautiful man—don't *be* anxious or depressed or anything else negative. That isn't who you are."

I took a moment to replay what he'd said. Words are powerful. Don't *be* anxious, or depressed, or desperate, or stressed, or any of a hundred other negative things I often thought about myself. I need to be careful with the words I use. *Have I really been defining myself this way? Could I be a new person if I just redefined myself with new words? Could it be that easy?*

Joe motioned for me to move closer to him and then he pointed to my heart. "You . . . right there! Who's in there?"

87

My seat just went from warm to hot underneath me as I looked down at his shaking finger pointing at me. "Well, apparently a little scaredy cat lives right there," I said with a laugh that I hoped would turn the topic to something else.

Joe smiled back and chuckled. "Well, what does that scaredy cat want? A bowl of milk?"

I laughed, but he clearly wasn't moving from this topic. "Well Joe, I just want my kids to be safe and secure. So I would say my passion is being a dad."

"Being a dad is a great passion, but 'safe and secure' sounds like what *fear* wants," Joe said as he grabbed my arm and directed my hand up to cover my heart. "Marcos, what does your heart want?"

I followed his direction and moved my hand over my heart.

"Go on," Joe prompted. "Ask it. Ask your heart what it wants."

I could feel my entire being swirling tightly around my familiar fear. "I don't know, Joe. It wants, it just wants to be okay."

Joe smiled and tilted his head at me as though I'd missed his lesson completely, then he jokingly made the sign of the cross in front of me as if I required exorcising. "Marcos, you *are* okay. If you are not ready to use those words for yourself yet, then I will say them for you. You are okay. Now, what does your heart want?"

I put my hand back over my heart and listened for the echoes of what used to live there. "Hmm, if I had all the money in the world, I would just want to hang out with my kids, love on my friends, maybe get back into dance again, maybe draw and paint. I love creating art with my kids."

I could see the wheels moving in Joe's head. "So, are you dancing? Are you creating art?"

I sank back into my chair. "Dancing? No way. Art? Just portfolio tuning work to try to get a job again."

Joe shook his head and let out a big breath. "Wow, so just work. Work, work, work, and nothing else?"

"Well, I do play the ukulele for fun," I said defensively. "I take one wherever I go."

Joe leaned in even further. "There it is!" he exclaimed. "Your face lit up just talking about the ukulele. Do you have one in your car?"

"Yes, I do."

"Go get it right now," he commanded. "Let's start with that."

Five minutes later, I walked through his front door playing and singing "I Can't Give You Anything (But My Love)" by the Stylistics. Joe laughed at the whimsical high sounds from my small wooden instrument and moved over on the couch to give me room to sit next to him.

"Are you going to serenade me?"

"I can't guarantee it will be any good," I replied as my hands strummed through a few chords until I landed on another song. "Here's one you'll know."

Joe swayed gently as I started singing "All of Me." I missed a chord or two and Joe had the right words when I didn't know a lyric in places. Joe didn't care and he grinned throughout the whole song.

"Wow! Marcos, that was great!" he said, reaching over to pat my hand. "An artist, a dance teacher, and a ukulele legend, you *are* an interesting person, Marcos. I would give you a golden buzzer if we were on TV. That little ukulele makes you so happy. Do you feel it?"

I did notice I had a sappy grin on my face. *Was I happy at that moment?*

"Quick, Marcos, get my phone," Joe demanded. "I want to take a picture of us. Use your long arm to take a picture of us. I will send it to you. I want you to see that smile and remember how happy your heart can be."

I snapped a selfie of us and looked at it. The image surprised me. "Oh man, look at me. I am actually happy."

"Yes, you are happy, Marcos," he said, making a point. "Just find something that makes your face look like that. It's that easy."

I put his phone back on the desk next to the computer. *How could it be easy? But who the hell would pay me to play the ukulele?*

"Come on, it's time for lunch," Joe urged. "After Perkins, I have a stop to make and someone to introduce you to."

Over lunch, Joe asked me about the songs I knew, how long I had been playing, and why the ukulele was so small.

"Have you ever taught anyone to play it?"

"I taught my son to play, but he prefers the guitar. He thinks it's way cooler."

"I don't know about that. Lots of people play the guitar, but you're the only ukulele player I know."

Joe paid the check and said his goodbyes to all the servers as I grabbed the cane and got him ready to leave. "What is this appointment we have this afternoon?"

"We're going to see my friend Marvin," Joe said, taking my hand to stand up out of the booth. "He cuts my hair and does my nails. He's such a wonderful young man. Marvin has a passion for helping people—he wants to become a nurse."

Good for him, I thought remembering the uncomfortable morning conversation after reading Tanya's email. *Everyone around Joe finds their passion, and I'm stuck with the ukulele.* "Give me the directions once we get to the car."

I paused with Joe by the pie case near the two sets of entry doors. There always seemed to be a traffic jam in the narrow glass corridor between the doors during lunchtime and I liked to walk Joe through alone to make it easier for us both. I was walking us over to our handicapped parking space, when my eyes caught the motion of a black BMW backing up aggressively and heading toward us. I stopped Joe with my left hand and waved his gnarled wooded cane in my right to get the driver's attention, but the driver kept coming at us. I hit his bumper hard with the rubber tip of the sturdy cane and that finally stopped him.

The driver sprang out of his car and started yelling at me. "What the hell are you doing? You hit my car!"

I don't think he even saw the old man I had moved behind me. "Dude! You were backing right into us."

He stormed right up to me, and I gripped the cane as a potential weapon as my adrenaline spiked.

"That's a seventy-thousand-dollar car!" he exclaimed as he turned to look at it. "If you dented it, I'll sue you."

I just stood looking at him, uncertain about what his next action would be.

"You're lucky, jackass!" he said as he got in his car and hit the gas, scraping the bottom in a loud crunch as he thundered out of the parking lot.

I looked down at Joe, who just said a long "Wow . . ."

"What a jerk! He could have hit us," I shouted, still feeling the panic tight in my throat.

"But he didn't," Joe said, squeezing my hand and leading me back on our course to the passenger door of my Mazda.

I sat Joe into the car and then got in and gripped the steering wheel as hard as I'd gripped the cane. "Where are we going again?" I demanded.

"To see Marvin," Joe said in a soothing voice. "To get my hair cut."

"Right."

"It's on University Boulevard, by the school. I'll show you."

We drove toward his appointment, but I couldn't let it go. "Do you believe that guy?"

"He must have really liked that car."

I looked at my mirrors again, still hyper-focused. "I was ready to let that guy have it. I wasn't going to let him hurt you."

"I know that, but we're okay now," Joe said, reaching over to pat my leg. "Don't give it another thought."

I smiled over at him, but my still-racing adrenaline wasn't done with me. I waited for a driver in front of us to get over so that we could continue. "Come on!"

Joe's laugh caught me off guard. "So, are you going to clobber him too?"

"I just might," I laughed and felt some of the tension escape. "The way my day's going, I just might." I pulled into the parking lot of the strip mall and took the first handicapped spot.

Joe reached over again and touched my leg. "Stop for a minute, Marcos. Do you see what just happened to you?"

"What? Do you mean shouting at that last driver? I was just venting."

"No, I mean the way you feel right now," Joe corrected. "Mr. Fancy Car was probably having a terrible day before we ran into him. Maybe he just lost his prestigious job that paid for that car? Maybe he just got served with divorce papers? We have no idea what caused him to be so angry, but we do know that he just passed that negative energy on to you. Do you notice how different you feel now compared to singing with your ukulele?"

I knew he was right. *Would he always be right?* "So what was I supposed to do?"

"You acted correctly, Marcos. You protected us. My question is, what should you do *now*? Don't let someone else put their bad day on you. You cannot control how you feel if you are letting others do it for you. Don't let someone else define you," he said with a brilliant smile. "Now, let's go see my friend Marvin."

I followed Joe's advice and tried to reset my feelings as I led Joe through the front door of the narrow and dated-looking salon. All the working stylists looked up from their different heads to smile and say hello to him.

"Joe Sabah! How are you, friend?" shouted a young Black man with a beautiful grin as he leaned over the woman in his chair. "Pam, dear, I just need a minute to get him settled."

The young stylist walked right up to Joe but kept his eyes on me. "You must be Joe's new caretaker. I'm Marvin. I'm Joe's favorite barber, his favorite nail tech, his favorite—"

"—everything," Joe and Marvin said at the same time and then laughed at what must have been an inside joke.

"I'm Marcos," I said, shaking his hand.

"Can I borrow our friend Joe?" Marvin asked, taking Joe's hand from me and expertly leading him. "I just need five more minutes with Pam. Let's sit you in Stacy's chair next to me."

Joe settled into the adjustable barber chair as Marvin's co-workers came by to say hi and chat with him.

"Joe, I have so much to tell you," Marvin said as he resumed clipping Pam's hair. "You know how we talked about me wanting to be a nurse? Well, I am moving back home to Baltimore to go to nursing school. I got accepted!"

"You're doing it!" Joe beamed. "Wow! That's great news. You are going to be an amazing nurse, Marvin."

Marvin turned the woman around in the chair to look at his finished work in the large mirror. "Well, what do you think?"

Pam just smiled and nodded as she admired her new look. "If you are half as good at nursing as you cut hair, you'll rock their world."

I looked over and Joe seemed nearly overwhelmed with joy for his friend. "Are you going to live with your mom?"

Marvin brushed the hair away from Pam's shoulders and removed the barber's cape. "I *have* to, Joe, the school is expensive. My mom is a *lot*, but we'll work it out."

"Being a mom is a lot," Joe answered with a wide smile. "She must love you to pieces. And she must be so proud of you, Marvin."

"All right, Ms. Pam, you are officially gorgeous," Marvin said, lifting Joe up and out of the neighboring chair with a confidence I was still searching for. "Joe, let's get started on you."

"We're doing the full show today, Marvin. Hair and nails."

"Sure thing," Marvin answered as he stroked Joe's remaining white hair to make it lie flat. "And no, you do *not* get a discount because you only have half your hair left to cut."

Both men smiled at what seemed like another shared joke.

"Give him a discount," urged the stylist two chairs down. "He's our best customer."

"I'll give you a discount if you come to me after Marvin leaves," shouted another barber from the end chair. "But none of that life-changing talk or the deal's off."

"Yeah, you could end up in Baltimore because of him!" All the stylists laughed in unison and it felt like Joe was the mayor of the barbershop too. *Was Joe the star of every place he went?* I thought and then instantly flashed back to my last conversation with Patrick, the previous caretaker, when I asked if Joe was some sort of celebrity. "Oh, you'll see," echoed in my ears again as I watched him light up the room.

Joe reached into his pocket and pulled out his black leather billfold as he motioned me to come to him. "Marcos," he said in a whisper over the chatter. "Can you take this money and go next door to the grocery store and get me some family packs of

Almond Joy and some more Ensures? We should be wrapping up by the time you get back."

I took the money but kept listening to their conversation as I walked to the door.

"It's true, Joe," Marvin said with some sadness as he cleaned and readied his equipment. "I won't be here next month."

"Then, we'd better make this one extra special," Joe sang out. "What was it you said to Ms. Pam? I want to be officially gorgeous too, so snap to it, Mr. Marvin."

I laughed with the rest of the shop as I pushed the door open and headed for the store.

I grabbed a red shopping cart and started toward the section that would have the two items that made up Joe's entire diet outside of Perkins lunches. Pushing the cart through the other shoppers, I couldn't help but notice the looks on their faces as they reached for items to place in their carts. They were blank and looked emotionless in their tasks. They seemed joyless compared to the bright, smiling, happy people I had just left at the salon across the parking lot. I steered my empty cart around stern mothers with pointing kids in tow and I stopped to check the curious sensation I was feeling as I paused my cart to let an oblivious man cut me off. It was contrast. I suddenly felt different. *Were these people around me in the store really different from the people I was used to meeting while caring for Joe? Or did that old man bring something different out of everyone around him?*

A stark feeling of isolation followed me and drove my thoughts as I collected the candy bars and nutritional drinks. No one smiled or interacted with anyone else. I tried to make eye contact with other shoppers, with the other people in my space, but their return looks made me feel more like an obstacle than an opportunity. *Was Joe's energy and positivity what was missing from this scene?* It felt like I had left a wonderful bubble as soon as I'd started walking across the parking lot toward the grocery store.

Pushing the cart toward the checkout lanes, I steered my sparse cart to the back of the longest one instead of instinctively choosing the shortest lane. I wasn't sure why I did it, but it did give me more time to watch the interactions of everyone around me. Half the store workers greeted guests as they started scanning their items while the others just started their tasks automatically. Coupon sorting and price checks were greeted with groans from the two shoppers ahead of me while necks craned to the right and left to look for shorter paths out. Everyone around me seemed so self-centered, so selfish, so small, *and* so uncomfortably famil- iar. The energy I felt from them brought me back to the familiar darkness of worry, fear, and self-pity that had defined my last six months. *Or had I held those defining feelings for longer than just the past half year?* I wondered as I pushed my cart to close up the gap as the woman behind me started placing her items on the belt behind me. *How could the contrast be that sharp already?* I had only been helping Joe for a few weeks. *Was I becoming more aware of the emotions around me because of Joe's lessons?*

I replayed Joe's words that had calmed me down after the incident with the driver. "Maybe the lady behind me had a bad day before she came to the store?" "Don't let other people put their bad energy on you." "*You* get to define how you feel." And then another conversation with Joe jumped into my mind as I removed his items from the cart. "You have to give before you get, Marcos." *If I wanted to get something more from the people around me—if I wanted something more like what I enjoyed feeling when I was with Joe—should I just give that first and see what happens?* That question brought me back to some of the first notes I had started capturing in my journal about how Joe treated people. *Was that part of his trick? Was that why he was so attractive?*

I stepped forward toward the twenty-something cashier as she silently handed the receipt to the man in front of me. "Hello," I said, addressing her directly and trying to make eye contact as I read her nametag. I wondered what her passion might be. "You guys are super busy today."

"It's been like this all day," she droned.

I imagined Joe standing beside me, poking his thumb in my back to do the next good thing as I presented his cash to her. "I am glad we have hard-working people like you to make this a pleasant experience for us. You're doing a great job, Sherry."

I looked back and noticed her curious eyes following me as I grabbed the two bags of items and walked toward the exit with a smile on my face.

"Marcos! You're back," Joe shouted above the contagious laughter filling the confines of the salon. "We were beginning to think we'd lost you."

"It's good to be back, Joe."

That night, I drove for double my normal time as I worked toward the goal of filling my balance with enough money to make the next mortgage payment. I waited for longer routes to pop up on the app. They paid more, but they also gave me more time with each rider—time I intended to use to practice some of the phrases and techniques I saw Joe using to create that bright bubble for all those around him.

"Hey, are you Jonathan? Hop in! I love that shirt. Is it vintage? Man, they don't make shirts that fit like that anymore. Holy cow, you designed it! I would love to see your work. Do you have a website?"

"Are you Anne? Are we waiting for anyone else? So, what kind of restaurant is it? Oh my god, I love tapas! So what was the occasion? A promotion, nice! What are you most excited about in your new role?"

"Hi, Kevin, how are ya? My night has been really good, thanks. I have had lot of great conversations. Tonight's topic keeps coming back to 'If you had all the money in the world, what would you do to make the biggest difference in people's lives?' I know, it is a good one."

CHAPTER 7

I arrived at Joe's apartment door and knocked lightly before letting myself in. After walking through the unused galley kitchen, I automatically started the morning routine of looking for his discreetly placed deposit bottles from the night before. I stepped into the living room and saw Joe sitting at the Macintosh with a smile on his face, waiting for me.

"Good morning, Marcos," Joe said with a sly smile that let me know something was up.

"Hello, Joe. How are you this morning?"

Joe inched to the edge of the office chair and reached out his hand for me to lift him up. "I'm a bit tired, to be honest," he said as he motioned for me to walk him over to the couch. "I worked on something last night and it's sort of a present to you."

"For me?" I asked as I lowered Joe into place and began my scan of the living room for the pee bottles that seemed curiously missing this morning.

"Oh, I straightened up a bit this morning so that you and I could get to some real work," Joe said as he motioned to the chair in front of the monitor. "Please take a look."

I placed my journal down on the desk and then sat down and looked at the monitor where I was surprised to see my own face looking out. It was the photograph from yesterday with me leaning into Joe while cradling my ukulele. I smiled when I saw Joe's welcoming grin, but I couldn't stop looking at my own image. It seemed to have a brightness and attraction that I hadn't seen in the mirror in a while. I lingered on the photo and it brought back the joy of yesterday's lunch with Joe. I moved my eyes up and saw the headline above the photo, "Ukulele Magic with Marcos Perez." My pulse jumped as my eyes darted to the text below the photograph:

> Learn to play the happiest of all musical instruments, the ukulele. My new friend and caretaker, Marcos Perez, will teach you how to play the ukulele either online or in person here in Denver. The first lesson is free and each lesson after that is $50 for one hour. Email me back to set up your first free lesson with Marcos. By the way, this could be a great way to warm up a crowd for your public speaking. Thanks, Joe Sabah

"What is this?" I asked, but kept my eyes locked on the screen. The email offer looked close to professional quality and I wondered how long Joe must have worked on it last night.

"It is a gift for you, Marcos."

"I don't understand, Joe. Do you intend to send this out to some of the people on your database list?"

"Not some, *all* of them," Joe countered with a satisfied smile.

"But that must be thousands of people."

"Fourteen thousand four hundred and sixteen," Joe corrected.

I pulled my wide eyes away from the screen and looked at Joe. "Why would you do this? I'm not ready for this."

Joe grinned. "Marcos, I saw you when you were playing for me yesterday. It was the happiest I have seen you. Just look at that smiling man in the photo next to me," Joe pointed to the screen. "Marcos, that instrument brings out something in you that is good, that is pure, that is joyous. It brings out something that you need to share with the world. And I thought it would be a way to make some extra money. When we send that email to my list, I know that two hundred people will respond, fifty will want a free lesson, and twenty will pay you to teach them. That's a thousand a month, but some might pay every week," he said with bright eyes.

"I can't do that!" I protested with a laugh as though it was a prank.

"Sure you can, Marcos," Joe stated as if it were a foregone conclusion. "You've just never done anything like this before."

I looked at the screen and imagined the pressure of teaching others. "No way. We can't send this."

Joe's warm face hardened into a fatherly resolve. "Why are you hiding?"

I shifted in the chair under the weight of Joe's question and turned to look at the email message again as I thought about an extra thousand dollars a month. "You're really planning to send this, aren't you?"

"Yes." He waited for me to turn back to him. "You need this," Joe stated with the confidence of a prescribing physician.

I reimagined the messaging going out to thousands of people, thousands of strangers, and the thought felt like a knot tightening inside of me. I had so much to do as it was. "No, I don't. What I need is to get my life on track again."

Joe inched forward on the couch cushion and locked his tender eyes on mine. "If we have something we are good at, something that brings us joy, something that lights us up, then we should be out there doing that thing. Each one of us has that something that is given to us as a gift to be shared, just like we spoke to Tanya about. Marcos, that is their purpose." Joe paused for a moment to emphasize his point.

"Marcos, we have only known each other a few weeks now, but I have been watching you closely. Yesterday with the uku-lele, I saw you light up for the first time. It was beautiful. You seemed to glow when you played for me," Joe said with a wide smile as if reliving the joy he had felt from me. He glanced at the monitor. "When I look at your face from yesterday, I can see that your ukulele is a gift that you need to share."

I watched him and tried to absorb his heartfelt words. "Joe, I appreciate that you thought of this for me." I turned back to the email and imagined the work that Joe must have put into it, working with his one good hand into the night to build it. "I appreciate what effort this must have been for you. But I can't do this."

"Marcos, sometimes these gifts challenge us and can seem scary," Joe continued. "They push us out of our little comfort areas when we don't want to be pushed and we hide from them. And hiding can be okay at first, but it is important to understand why we are hiding."

Joe leveled his eyes at me again. "Why are you hiding?"

I flashed back to the interview in this living room two weeks ago, where Joe had asked the same question twice—the second time trying to get to a deeper meaning. I sat with Joe's question for a moment before answering. "I don't feel like I am hiding from anything, I'm just not sure I'm a ukulele teacher."

Joe smiled but kept his serious tone. "You can do anything. You've got talents, Marcos, and more than just the ukulele. I see them in you. You need to be out there, sharing those things with the world." Joe directed his eyes to the desktop next to the Macintosh. "What are you writing in that journal you carry around with you?"

I covered the journal defensively with my hand. "I just capture notes, concepts, and ideas. Sometimes I sketch in it when I want to capture a moment."

Joe brightened, as though he could see something that I could not. "There you go, you should write a book then."

I thought about the past year of dark thoughts and personal passages captured on the pages now trapped under my protecting hand. They were hardly topics of inspiration worthy of sharing with others.

"Perhaps you could become a speaker, like Tanya, or the hundreds of others I've trained. You could tell the story of you and Elliott, and his journey. I bet a lot of people would like to hear that one."

I shook my head and gave a nervous laugh. "Ah, we're still very much in process on that front." I thought about the worn journal and the passages they contained about Elliott and my struggles as a father to both Elliott and departed Ella. *Perhaps I was hiding from that.* I rested on that thought for a moment until Joe spoke again.

"Why are you here?" Joe asked as he leaned back into the couch as if to give space for the answer.

It was an open and comfortable-sounding question this time and I relaxed in the chair as I sensed Joe had moved on from grilling me more on the hiding question. "That's the third time you've asked me that."

Joe just smiled and nodded back at me.

"I don't want to miss this answer three times," I said, smiling back. "During our first interview, Patrick did the talking and then asked you if you wanted to ask your question and you asked me that, twice. What do you mean when you ask people that?"

"Patrick is right. It is a question I use a lot," he chuckled in his thin voice, "but not everyone is prepared or comfortable answering it. Basically, it is what do you think you are supposed to be doing in life? Is there something in your life, like art, or graphic design, or playing the ukulele that gives you so much pleasure and joy that you just want to pour yourself into it and would do it whether anyone paid you or not? You are a father, a musician, and a dancer, but are you singing the song you came here to sing?"

The question hung in the air between us in his sparse living room and it offered me a moment to reflect on listening for any joy in my life as I might hear a song. I couldn't remember hearing anything like that in at least six months. No, it felt like longer than that. I remembered hearing it in short measures when I held the ukulele, or a drawing pencil, or my daughter in a dance frame, but even those sounded like faint echoes bouncing down into a dark well.

"Do you have it?" Joe asked with anticipation.

I lingered in the moment a bit longer before answering. "I think I hear just enough of it to remind me that it's missing. It feels like it's playing in another part of the building, like it's playing for someone else."

Joe leaned forward again. "That's okay. That's good, so long as you can hear it and recognize it. That is enough to start."

"What about you?" I countered, eager to move the focus from myself. "What is Joe Sabah's song?"

A wide grin crept over Joe's face, as though he had a gift to give. "Turn around," he prompted, "and look at our announcement."

I turned and looked at his joyous face in the posting again as Joe continued. "All those names next to the emails, all those people who might still get a free ukulele lesson if they're lucky," Joe laughed and continued, "All of those people came to me with the same dream of talking to groups of people to share their stories with others. Each one of them is like a song to me. Some are fast songs, and some are slow. Some are happy songs, some are sad ones. Each of them is unique and deserves to be brought out and heard."

I scanned through a few dozen names on the list. "This is a lot of songs."

"And I'm not done yet," Joe said with a joyous confidence that still crackled through his speech when he was excited. "Patrick is the latest song."

"Patrick? Really?"

Joe's head rose and fell in a solemn nod. "Patrick's wife has cancer. It's bad and she might not survive. They want to spend their remaining time focusing on the joy they bring each other, instead of the fear that each of them faces. Patrick and I talked about that for a long time and that's why Patrick had to step away from me, and that is what led you and me together, Marcos. This is why Patrick and I laughed in your interview and why I said you were perfect. You might be my next song, Marcos," Joe laughed.

"I might be more work than you're ready for," I laughed as I tried to match Joe's warm smile.

"We'll see," Joe said, inching to the edge of the couch and extending his right arm for me to help him up. "Wow! What a morning we've had. Let's get ready to go to lunch."

I sighed with relief that his change of topic might mean Joe was done with his motivational prodding this morning. "What should we do with this email message?" I asked.

"I won't send the message if you don't want me to," Joe said, getting to his feet, "but I won't delete it either. You do what you want with it. You're the assistant, you delete it."

I helped Joe over to his cane and he shuffled down the hallway to get ready to leave. I returned to the computer monitor and reread the Ukulele Magic email again. Moving the mouse in my hand, I gauged the emotions I felt when the cursor moved back and forth between the send and the delete icons until Joe emerged from his bedroom.

I grabbed his Mayor of Perkins pin that served as the final systems check before our daily departure and I clicked SAVE on the message and closed the file. "Are you ready?" I asked.

Joe nodded and reached out his right hand to me, but as we walked together through the kitchen to the front door of the apartment, I could feel a change come over Joe. His worn back straightened slightly and his crooked frame stiffened with some newfound resolve. Joe pulled back on my leading hand for a moment as he looked up into my eyes. "We have so much good to do today, Marcos. Let's go!"

I felt a rush of fresh strength in Joe's hand and I tried to imagine that source of energy and hope that he could tap at will. I looked down and marveled that this look of summoned determination fit him—like some wounded superhero who was still able to throw on the cape and fly. Joe squeezed my hand as he took his first stride into the day.

I parked the car with enough space on the passenger side so that Joe could get out easily when I offered him a supporting hand to help him out and onto his feet.

"We nailed the dismount," Joe joked as he gripped me and steadied himself on his feet.

I smiled and started leading him to the entrance. I had grown to dread the glass double entry doors as a sort of obstacle course of human traffic that I had to navigate Joe through twice a day. With the instincts of a dance teacher leading a student away from oncoming couples, I measured Joe's steps across the parking lot, always keeping an eye on the people getting ready to enter and exit the restaurant so that we might arrive at the glass gauntlet without a crowd.

I felt good about our timing until a truck full of construction workers stopped in one of the parking spaces close to the door and four men bounded out and were now on an intercept course with us at the front door. I pulled back on Joe's hand a bit to slow our pace, but Joe kept his shuffle-stride rhythm going until all six of us were at the door at the same time. I could sense the urgency in the men, as though they had only a short window to get their lunches. "Let's wait for a second and let these guys through," I whispered, but Joe ignored me and kept going as the lead worker held open the outer door on his side.

I forced a smile and nodded to the man as we entered with the other co-workers and then all six of us ran right into a family of five that pushed through the inner doors, eager to exit. I took a leading step to the side to guide Joe out of the traffic, but Joe slowed his pace in a way that made him instantly seem feebler and more vulnerable than he really was. Seeing the face of the oncoming father, I knew that look of focus and determination when a father becomes a herder.

Joe seemed oblivious to the tension at first and then he came to a full stop right in the middle of the nine strangers. The effect on everyone around him was striking. Joe became like a statue in the narrow entryway, and everyone turned their attention to him. He seemed to expand and slowly fill the glass foyer as though he held some intention for them. Joe turned, looked up, and acknowledged each waiting face as he spoke to them in a slow sequence. "You guys are great. You are so patient and helpful, I just love coming to this place for lunch," he croaked in a voice so thin now that I barely recognized it, "Thanks for helping me do this today."

I shifted my gaze from the father of the family to see the immediate effect Joe's plea had on the others. Each face softened and filled with compassion as they stepped back and held open the doors. "Happy to help." "Come on through, sir." "Enjoy

109

your lunch," each stranger offered in turn. I watched in stunned amazement as these harried strangers parted and ushered him through the doors like an aged king entering his court.

Joe smiled at them as they went on their way and then he turned his now confident face back up to me. "It's that easy," he said in his normal voice again and winked before starting to walk at his normal pace again over to his usual booth.

"What the heck was that, Joe?" I said as I reflected on the effects of that staged scene in the entryway.

Joe grinned with the confidence of a master. "Everyone has goodness in them, Marcos. Once you know it's there, your job is to see it and point to it. That's what that was," he said, turning a bit to the left to be able to see the door better.

"Hi, Dad!" came a voice that turned both of our heads around. It was one of the servers. She was tall, in her mid-thirties, and wore a black half apron tight around her waist.

"Twyla," Joe beamed. "How is my favorite server?" he whispered as she stopped at the booth. "Twyla, this is Marcos. He is my new assistant."

"So nice to meet you, Marcos," she started before I could reply. "I want you to take good care of Joe here. He's my dad, my Denver dad. My real dad lives in Daytona," she continued, "but Joe here is more of a dad to me than he was."

"How are your kids doing, Twyla?" Joe asked. "And what about Willow's English class troubles? Did my tip help her?"

I watched her face brighten. "The kids are great and yes, she is doing much better now. Who would have imagined just reading it out loud could make her writing so much better."

"Wow! That's great. Just great," Joe said. "How about Jenny, is she starting to make more friends?"

"We're working on it. It's getting better," she answered and then turned to me. "What can I get started for you to drink?"

"I'll have a Diet Coke," I answered her, "but let's get his order first."

Twyla laughed. "I already know his order, 'coffee, two creams,'" she said in unison with Joe as he did his two-fingered double tap on the table. "Coffee, two creams, and a Diet Coke coming right up," she said, walking off.

"Twyla is amazing," Joe started. "She raises two kids by herself and now she is taking classes at night on management. She will be a great manager if she sticks with it. I see her helping the newer staff members all the time. She will be an assistant manager here before long. Working with people is her song." Joe said, turning a bit to the left to be able to see the door better. "We are expecting another to join us today. There he is," Joe pointed and waved. "His name is Monty, he is a long-time student of mine. He has been speaking full-time for a few years now."

"Do you want me to go and bring him here?"

Joe laughed and shook his head. "He knows the way. All of them know the way. This is *my* booth. Everyone knows I will be here," he said, turning in the other direction in the booth to greet his student. "Monty! Wow! So good to see you. Monty, this is Marcos, he's my new assistant."

"Hello, Marcos," said Monty. He was middle-aged and looked very fit under his freshly pressed dress shirt. He shook my hand and turned back to Joe, "No Patrick today?"

Joe pursed his lips and shook his head slightly. "Patrick is spending more time with his wife these days."

Monty nodded and turned back to me, "Welcome to Team Sabah, where it's either a rewarding pat on the head when you get better, or a motivating thumb in the back until you do."

Joe threw his head back and laughed. "Am I really so tough?"

"Well, it never seems that way when we start," Monty answered and shot a glance back over to Joe, "but . . ."

"So what will it be today, Monty?" Joe chuckled. "Why don't you start by telling me all the wonderful things that have happened in your speaking career as a result of doing what you said you would do last time? Did you call all the radio show producers on the list?"

"I called several of them, but then I thought about a different type of outreach."

"How many did you call?" Joe interrupted.

Monty tensed up a bit and framed his answer. "I called about a dozen, but there's this new idea I have about just mailing them my bio along with my expertise topics."

"You called a dozen? That's it? My list has over six hundred producers on it, you have to call all of them," Joe said sternly, all of the old-man charm now gone. "Mailing is fine, but only after you call and talk to them. Getting speaking exposure is about relationships. What kind of relationship are you going to build through a letter or an email?" Joe challenged.

"I did get two radio spots and three paid in-person speaking jobs since our last meeting," Monty said, trying to change the topic to something positive that Joe could focus on.

"Wow! That's great Monty. I want to hear about those successes, but after we finish old business. Monty, my system works," Joe emphasized. "That system built the careers of Douglas and Stern and it still works now—if you work it. You have to make the calls so that the producers know you. Will you start calling them again?" Joe asked and then sat quietly, waiting for a response.

Monty sat and looked at Joe before turning to me as if to say, *I told you so.*

I thought back to the ukulele lesson conversation of that morning and said nothing, secretly cheering on the inside that Joe had his thumb in someone else's back.

Monty turned back to Joe and nodded. "Yes, I will start calling again."

"Great! Wonderful!" Joe said with a smile before countering. "What day next week will you start calling them?"

"What day?"

"Yes, what day?" Joe asked before turning to me. "Marcos, can you get your journal out and take note of what day next week Monty will be restarting his calls? I want to set up a phone call in my system to call Monty and check in at the end of next week."

Monty sighed and surrendered to his mentor. "Joe, I will start calling on Monday and we can sync up on Friday."

"Wow! That's great," Joe interrupted before Monty could continue. "How many local clubs and associations did you reach out to since our last meeting?"

Monty took a deep breath and began recalling his recent outreach.

I paid attention to Joe's consultation with Monty for a while but eventually looked away from their conversation and back to the people coming and going through the glass-walled entryway. Their faces looked normal again, like the way the family and construction workers looked before Joe stopped and brought out the best in them. *It's that easy.* I repeated the words in my mind and snuck a quick glance back at Joe. I had felt those strangers change in that moment. It *was* like a magic trick. But Joe did that trick with everyone. He did it with Twyla the server, with Marvin the manicurist, with Sophie the barber, with Steve the manager, and with Monty in the booth next to me. That trick was like a charmed bubble of positivity that circled him wherever he went. Now that I had seen it, I knew that I wanted it. I replayed the way each stranger had responded with a bright, welcoming warmth to Joe and I imagined people reacting to me that way.

Thinking back to the apprehension I felt walking with Joe as we approached the crowded doors, that reluctance wasn't because I was looking for opportunities to engage with people to try to highlight the goodness in them, it was something else. It was fear. It was hiding.

It's that easy. I heard Joe's words again in my mind. *What if he's right?* I thought. *What if it is as easy as just searching for the goodness in everyone and then recognizing and acknowledging it when you see it? Is that all there is to his trick? Is that how he does it? Is that all it might take to be able to do it?* I stayed on that thought for a long time and tried to envision how things could be different if it were that easy. But the more I thought, the more I realized that I was doing the exact opposite. By focusing on how bad everything was, I was missing things in front of me that were going right. I sat in the booth next to them and thought about Elliott and his transition, but all I could see was how *my* fear had tainted and hampered that journey. I heard my own words to Elliott echoing back to me, "that will be so hard," "they will make fun of you," and "what will Nanna and Pappa think?" *Was I hampering him when I thought I was helping?* I tried to think back to all the good things Elliott had done along the way that I hadn't recognized or acknowledged.

I looked out the window at people who passed as I thought about the challenges that awaited Elliott: the confusion and hateful looks he would get from something as simple as being called out for using the wrong bathroom, dating and finding love, the estrangement of the gender checkbox on a job application. I thought about what kind of confidence it would take for a transgender adult to navigate that minefield, and then I thought about the confidence it would take to do that as a teenager still in high school.

How much better equipped would Elliott be if I could just see the good in him and the goodness in the pursuit of his truth? How much easier would it be for him if I could just start looking for those positive things and point to them? How much happier would Elliott be? How much happier would Lilly and I be? I stared out the window and felt the emotion rising when I thought about Elliott's courage. The boy knew the hardships and challenges a transgender life would present him. Elliott had already suffered violence at the hands of intolerant classmates and he had endured hatred so strong that suicide had seemed safer than living. I thought Elliott must harbor the same fear of that formidable future that I felt and yet he had the bravery and strength to walk a path that was true for him. *How good was that?* I thought as my eyes filled with tears of regret that I had not embraced Elliott and crushed him close in recognition of that goodness.

I wanted to leave the restaurant and find Elliott right then to hug him and tell him I was proud of him. I wanted to stand up and walk to him now and tell him that I would stand by his side and protect him on his journey. I wanted to race out of the building and exclaim that I loved him, but Monty sat in my way and had paid for this hour with Joe. I sat back and reflected on what felt like an important lesson from Joe and I resolved never again to miss a moment like that. I resolved there in the restaurant, in that booth next to Monty, that I would find out if it could be as easy as Joe made it look. I resolved to look for the goodness in Elliott and in others, perhaps even within myself.

"Isn't that right, Marcos?" asked Joe.

The question jolted me back into the booth and the conversation between Joe and Monty. "I'm sorry, Joe. I was lost in my own thoughts for a moment. What was that?"

"We were just finishing here and I was just reminding Monty that the Colorado Speakers Association meeting is tonight and that I will be there. You can take me there, right?"

I thought about Elliott and about Lilly and how much I wanted to see them both right then, but they were with their mother until Saturday. "Sure, Joe. I'd love to."

I helped Joe up and out of the car and then reached down to straighten his loosely knotted, 1970s-era tie.

"Thanks for agreeing to bring me here early. I like to get one of the good seats. Let's go," Joe commanded with excitement as we started to walk toward the Tudor-styled, brick and wood beam country club building.

I had driven by the Wellshire Country Club many times but had never been inside. I helped Joe through the massive carved oak doors that gave way to what I had imagined a country club would look like, wood-paneled walls, exposed beams spanning lofty ceilings.

"The meeting will be in the main room down this hall," Joe said, turning us both.

"This place looks nice," I said, looking at the art and photographs of members on the walls.

"I like coming here," Joe replied with a wide smile. "I picked this place when I started this association over thirty years ago."

"Wait," I asked as we walked into a great hall with double-height ceilings and elegant rows of gothic arched stained glass windows along all three exterior walls, "you started this?" Twelve round tables with chairs dotted the expanse of the room that anchored around a speaker's podium.

"I did," he said, pausing at the opening to the room. "That was a long time ago, but it feels like just last week."

"There he is!" came a shout from across the room that drew their attention. "Right down in front, mister," bellowed a tall, heavyset man from the front of the room.

"Thomas!" Joe replied at his full volume.

"Joe, we're placing you right here," the large man said as he walked to the center table and pulled back a chair.

I navigated Joe through the field of tables and chairs toward the front. "Thomas, so good to see you. This is Marcos, my new assistant. Marcos, this is Thomas. He is the current chair of the association, so technically our host for tonight. He is also a very popular speaker who tours, isn't that right?"

"When they call me, I do," Thomas laughed. "Are you still getting on the radio, Joe?"

"Oh yes. Two shows last month," Joe said as they approached his place of honor. "I'm not done yet!"

"Good for you, Joe, or should I say, Wow!" he said as Joe joined in on the last word and they both laughed. "Nice to meet you Marcos and thank you for helping our Joe."

"It's my pleasure," I replied, "but I'm not sure who's helping who at this point."

118

"That's the way it works with this one," Thomas said as he rested a hand on Joe's shoulder. "Joe, I need to go finish setting up and greeting our members tonight," he said before stepping away to meet the gathering crowd.

One by one, and in groups of two and three, most of the older speakers in attendance stopped and sat with Joe to share a memory of the past or a recent accomplishment. I listened to their stories and occasionally received their thanks as though I now safeguarded a treasure for them. Joe reveled in this attention from these aspiring and professional speakers that he still considered his peers. I stayed at the table with him and stepped away only to bring water and small plates of appetizers to keep Joe and his company going. On one trip back with more plates, I overheard three guests talking about Joe and I lingered to listen.

"Who is that man over there that people are talking to?" asked an older man, who was rail-thin and as tall as I was.

"That's Joe Sabah," answered a tall, middle-aged woman in a white dress who stood next to two other men. "He is a bit of a legend around here. He started this Colorado branch a long time ago. Poor fella had a stroke a few years ago."

"Joe worked with the best back in the day," interjected an older man with a cane in a gray sport coat standing next to her. "Joe knew and worked with legends like Zig Ziglar, Og Mandino, even Norman Vincent Peale."

"Wait, the Power of Positive Thinking guy?"

The woman and both men looked at the thin man and nodded in unison.

"Joe worked with them, but he really helped them with promotion," said the second man in the bolo tie. "When Ziglar would tour, say back in the 1970s, Zig would call Joe and ask him to help him sell five hundred tickets and Joe would agree, and then Ziglar's team would mail him 1,500 tickets. Joe sold them all, every time. That is how he got his start. He was a master of promotion back then."

"Some would say he still is today," countered the woman. "He still mentors people and consults and I think he still teaches a class on public speaking, bless his heart."

"Yes, he teaches a course on how to start speaking. I guess some people still find it useful," said the bolo tie.

"He's got a good way with people," the woman answered, "and his work keeps him going. Just look at him, he's eighty-seven."

I looked over at Joe who was showing off his cane to two of the younger attendees as I drifted from their conversation and quietly placed the small plates of snacks within reach of Joe's right hand, giving Joe his space to enjoy his time but always keeping a watchful eye on him. I moved away to mingle with clusters of others who stood and milled about shaking hands and making new introductions around the room. After an hour, the homages to Joe had trickled to a stop and now the entire hall was buzzing with standing conversations in different parts of the room. I looked over and saw Joe sitting alone and that is when I nodded politely until I could break away from my conversation. I watched Joe as he sat alone and looked longingly at a crowd he had started but could no longer keep up with. It was as though he knew he could still stop by and reminisce, but it had all passed him now.

I walked up and sat in the chair next to him as I pulled a nutritional shake from my pocket, opened it, and placed it in front of him. Joe looked happy but was too exhausted to speak. "One for the road, Joe?" I asked as I pushed the shake in front of him. Joe took a sip and then nodded. "Let's get you home, Joe," I said with a warm smile, "it's time for bed."

CHAPTER 8

"Why are you hiding, Marcos?" I woke up before sunrise with Joe's challenge still filling my ears. I hadn't applied for a job in weeks and I would have to hand in a job search report to Phil next week to continue my unemployment benefits. *Maybe I was hiding from some things.*

I walked down into the basement and started the computer, determined at least to stop hiding from the dreaded daily search. After an hour of looking, I found three interesting postings: senior designer at an advertising agency, senior graphic designer at a Christian college, and graphic designer at a Buddhist university in nearby Boulder, Colorado. I pulled up all three listings side by side and imagined myself coming out of hiding and working on the tasks in each job description. The ad agency was closest to what I had been doing and I imagined it would pay the best, but the other two were more interesting to me. Both positions were heading up the design of school newsletters and alumni magazines, which sounded like less stress than advertising, but less money too. *Any money would be more than I was bringing home now by driving every night.*

Both educational positions offered tuition assistance that could be a path to a master's degree. That was a very attractive benefit, I thought, but I instantly felt like it had been a long time since I had allowed myself to think about distant goals of graduate school and becoming a therapist.

I hit the apply button on each one and started putting in my information and attaching resumes and portfolios, but stopped when each posting offered an optional cover letter to the application.

I thought about what to include in a cover letter and the only thing that came into my mind was Joe's question from my home care interview—*"why are you here?"* I imagined each potential employer would ask the same question if I got the chance to sit in front of them, so I determined to answer it up front. Opening three new document files, I knew that I needed to show my passion for artistic work as a driver for applying. But after a few opening sentences, I slowed to a stop before the blinking cursor. *Come on, Marcos,* I said to myself over the quiet in the basement. *Why do you want this? Find the words.*

My memories flashed back to sitting with Joe in his apartment where his challenging words came back to me: "What does your heart want?" I sat back in the chair and took in a deep meditative breath. *I'm okay.* Then I instinctively raised my right hand to cover my heart as I had done the first time, and then I listened. The answer was ready this time and I was shocked as the words poured out onto the three pages in a rush that revealed a dormant creative passion that now wanted to wake up. After less than an hour, I had three unique cover letters— each one answering why I wanted to be there. *At least I'm not hiding from this,* I whispered to myself as I clicked submit on each one.

I arrived at Joe's apartment with a confident stride from feeling like I had accomplished something even though I had only added three more positions to a long list of unanswered applications. I let myself in and called out to Joe, who called back from the couch. "Good morning, Marcos."

"Good morning, Joe. How are you this morning?' I asked. "That was quite an event last night."

"And I loved every minute of it. Thanks for taking me there and staying with me," Joe answered as he rubbed his hands together in what looked like a request for a hot cup of tea. "I hope you enjoyed it."

I started to work on two cups for us. "I *did* enjoy it. I learned some things too—like you're sort of famous, Joe. Everyone there knew you."

"Well, I did start it," Joe said with pride.

"I overheard some people talking about you," I said as I brought in his tea. "Did you really know Zig Ziglar and Norman Vincent Peale?"

"Yes, I knew them. I worked with them as well. I worked with Og Mandino too. Og made everyone laugh. They were all great speakers, true giants, and I learned a lot from them. They paved the way for generations of public speakers to follow."

"Were you a public speaker?"

"I was, but it became hard for me to stand up long enough to deliver my messages," Joe said, reaching his right hand over to touch his left leg. "That's when I started teaching it."

"How many people have you taught?"

Joe sipped his tea as he thought about my question. "Thousands. I've taught all kinds of people to be public speakers. You can speak about anything, even you could do it. The first step to speaking is writing," Joe said, pointing to my leather journal. "I see you scribbling in that thing all the time. What was it you said you write about? Notes, thoughts, ideas?"

"This is just my journal," I answered defensively. "Lately, I've been writing about you."

Joe looked at me with a serious look on his face. "Well, there you go. You should write about that as a way to get your creativity into the world."

"I'm not a writer. What am I going to do, start a blog?" I laughed. "I barely post things on social media."

"Do that then," Joe urged. "Just get something out of that journal and into the world to get you started. Can you do that?"

I can do that, I thought. *I could let people know about this interesting man.* "Sure Joe, I'll do it."

"See? That wasn't so hard, was it? Who knows, you might be a writer after all," Joe said with a smile that quickly disappeared as his praise turned to expectation. "I can't wait to see what you create."

I looked over at Joe, who seemed satisfied that he had already started his motivating for the day. *I should tell people about him,*

I thought as I felt a tingle of excitement as ideas started to form around what I could write.

"Who knows," Joe started. "If you write about me, it might bring me more business."

I laughed as I captured a few ideas for the social media post in my journal and wondered, *how much more business do you need when you're nearly ninety?*

During our lunch at Perkins, I prompted Joe to tell me stories about working with famous speakers and how he started the Colorado chapter of the National Speakers Association. I loved seeing his eyes blaze with excitement as he relived those events and reminisced about those relationships.

As I walked him back to the car, he stopped near our parking spot and turned to me. "You're walking different today. What's going on? Did you meet a girl?"

I laughed out loud as I turned to him. "No. Joe, could you really see me asking a woman out right now? Hi, I'm unemployed, broke, and a bit of a bummer—do you want to hang out?"

Joe waved off my self-deprecating joke. "That's just hiding."

"I did start applying for artistic jobs again. I applied for three interesting ones this morning."

"That's it!" Joe said as we started walking again. "Tell me about them on the drive back."

"Sure," I said, checking the ground for debris or liquids before easing him into his seat.

125

"Three jobs? Wow!"

"There is this advertising agency that I have always wanted to work for and I know they pay their creatives very well."

"Cha-ching," Joe said, rubbing his fingers against his thumb.

"The other two are both colleges, nonprofits, so I don't expect the pay to be so hot—but they do offer free tuition, so I could work there and get my master's degree."

"What degree do you want to get?" Joe asked.

"A master's in psychology. I've always dreamed of becoming a therapist and being able to help kids overcome challenges through art."

"A therapist?" Joe asked in an excited voice. "Marcos, that could be the song you are supposed to be singing. Tell me about why you want to help kids with art."

Thinking about his question, I started to feel something rekindle deep inside of me, like a part of me was waking up after a long sleep. "My favorite thing in the world is creating art with my kids. Whether it's just creating music, or dancing, or picking up bones in the forest for experimental projects—I love creating and seeing my kids blossom and grow through anything artistic." My words, spoken out loud at last, resonated deep within me. *Was Joe right about this being my song?* "Art has helped us get through some challenging times, I guess I imagined it could help other families as well."

"That's it, Marcos!" Joe shouted. "Ditch the money from the posh advertising firm and follow that dream. Can you imagine how many youngsters you could help?"

My eyes began to well up as I allowed myself to revisit this long-shelved dream.

"Get that degree man! Tell me about these schools, Marcos." Joe urged.

"Well, the first one is a Christian school, Coronado Christian College. They are looking for a senior designer to conceptualize their outreach advertising. I looked at some of their recent material and they could certainly use some of my help. The other school is a Buddhist university in Boulder, which would mean a longer drive. It's called Naropa. I've known some people who have gone there, and they love it. They teach a type of meditation that I have used for a few years now. It's smaller than Coronado, but I think it's sort of cooler and more interesting. They offer courses and a degree in art therapy."

"That could be the one, Marcos."

It could be, I thought as I drove us. The idea really resonated with me.

"Wait a second," Joe continued. "You said that you applied for these jobs, right?"

"I did apply, this morning."

"Did you ask for the job?" Joe asked.

"What do you mean? Like did I ask in the cover letter?"

"No," Joe said, shaking his head. "Pull the car over, please. This is important."

"But I'm driving."

"Yes, and I want you to stop driving. Pull over right there," Joe said, pointing to the empty parking lot in front of a Syrian restaurant.

I pulled in, parked, and looked over at Joe who was already staring at me in what felt like a meaningful moment. "Marcos, did you ask him?" he challenged as he pointed a bony finger up to the sky.

My eyes followed his finger to the roof of the car, but the practice of looking up into a blank space overhead brought me back to my frustrated outburst toward God that started me doing the next good thing. "Joe, I think God knows that I need a job."

Joe smiled as he had anticipated that response. He reached his weathered right hand over and touched my knee as he looked me in the eye. "Seek and you shall . . ."

"Find," I answered.

"Ask and you shall . . ."

"Receive."

His eyes teared up a little as if he knew I was close to something. "So ask him, ask the universe, ask a higher power, but ask."

My driver's seat suddenly felt more like a church pew, and I said a small prayer to myself at that moment.

Joe touched my knee again. "Speak it out loud. There is power in your words."

My mouth felt stuck, but I could feel the words forming in my throat. "God, I want that job," I said, visualizing the redbrick buildings of the small Buddhist university. "I want to be a therapist," I added as I started to choke up.

Joe reached up and grabbed my hand. "It only works if you ask out loud. I know that's not always easy. Good work, Marcos."

I turned my face a bit to the left to try to get my emotions in check.

128

"Ya know, he's your dad. He wants you to be happy."

I laughed, but I couldn't look over at him without getting emotional again. "Okay, Joe, I hope so." The request felt different now and something inside me knew that Joe was right. Saying it out loud made it more real, like I was claiming it for myself.

After I got Joe home, all he wanted to talk about was preparing me for the interviews he was sure I would get. "I hope you're right, but it's been six months and you are the only one to give me an interview," I joked.

"And it's a good thing I did," Joe countered with a laugh as he settled in on the couch and placed his walking cane against the armrest. "You need to get the right mindset for when they call. I wrote a whole book on how to get the job you really want. I'll coach you on what to do. I see your song in one of those jobs and positivity is the key to getting it."

"What are you talking about?" I asked.

"Marcos," Joe said, looking at me very seriously. "I love you, I really do, you're an amazing man, but you are not always the most positive and upbeat guy."

"Thanks?" I answered in an unsure tone. "I think there was a compliment in there somewhere."

"Marcos," Joe continued. "You're harder on yourself than you should be, and you sometimes need to be reminded of how great you are. And a job interview, even over the phone, is about making a first impression that is so attractive that they want more of you. Do you think that's where you are right now?"

129

His question struck me like a punch. *Most days* I *didn't want more of me.* I paused my first defensive answer as I replayed how I always felt in Joe's company. *I wanted more of him—everyone did.* The transition from the salon to the grocery store and back showed me what he could do with people was real. *I wanted that for myself and now was my opportunity.* I closed my eyes and quietly asked for it.

"Ooh, you are so right. I really need your help. How do you do it?"

Joe looked at me and smiled with pride. "It's easy," he said. "It's just a few simple things followed by a lifetime of practice."

I was hoping for something a little more immediate, I thought as I grabbed my journal again and flipped to the first blank page as Joe began to speak.

"First remember that positive always beats negative, always. So think of something positive to say for each first interview so that you pique their interest. For example, you said you reviewed the Christian college's content and that they could use your help. Instead, say that you loved something in their last magazine cover and that you have an idea to take that to the next level."

I nodded and wrote as fast as I could.

"Can you think of a compliment for the Buddhists in Boulder?"

I looked up from my notes and thought about their content that I had reviewed. "I can. They use a lot of Eastern symbolism in their content so that you know what kind of school you are looking at, but they do it in a way that doesn't make you feel like you are walking into a monastery with monks in orange robes. It's not bad."

"Ugh, Marcos," Joe interjected. "Watch your language. You just said *not* and *bad* in a three-word sentence. Listen to how that sounds. When you do that, you are sending negative messages to others. Positive beats negative. Try rewording phrases like 'no problem,' 'no worries,' 'not bad,' 'nothing to it,' 'no complaints,' and probably my least favorite, 'no sweat.' It may seem like a small thing, but it is a big thing. Practice it for a while."

"I will, Joe," I said as I wrote down the negative phrases to watch for.

"And instead of saying you can't do something or that you have never done something they ask you about—turn it around and beat that negative with a positive like, I helped someone do that, or I've always wanted to accomplish that, or building a campaign like that is a goal I look forward to completing. People love to hear that and what's more, they love to help people reach their goals."

"I like that."

"Next, you need to share with them what excites you about their opportunity. People hire passion and potential as much as they hire ability and experience. Let your excitement for something be a big positive."

"Well, I'm certainly excited about the tuition help and being able to go to grad school while I work."

"Share *that* with them! This lets them know you plan to stay around and contribute for a while and that you value their school enough to invest your valuable time," Joe said and then leaned toward me. "By the way, I'm excited about that too."

I had been thinking of going back to school since I first saw the two university job postings. "Joe, I really hope this going back to school thing can work, but I worry about the pay. Being broke as I get a master's degree sounds miserable."

Joe sat back and listened as I talked myself through the scenarios that had been running through my head since before breakfast. "Maybe the advertising job would be better. I know what they pay and my family needs the money right now. I'm good at it and I've been doing it forever."

Joe kept his eyes on me and waited for me to continue down my track. When I paused, he just raised his right hand and said, "But . . ."

His prompt was like hitting a start button on an anxiety motor as I began to relive the stress of my old job. "But the work is crazy and so cutthroat sometimes. Everyone loves their own ideas and creative sessions can turn ugly when people start fighting to keep their visions alive. It's like you give birth to something precious and you fall in love with it and what you think it can become or accomplish. The idea becomes your little baby, but there can only be one idea that gets made—so out come the daggers until only one remains."

"Marcos, that sounds terrible. That doesn't sound like you. That doesn't sound like a job that you want. Frankly, it doesn't sound like you enjoyed that work when it was your *last* job." Joe turned to face me and emphasize his points. "Do work that you are passionate about. Be yourself, Marcos. Don't hide behind some lie you told yourself."

He was right, of course. The returning pain in my stomach notified me of that, even if *I* wasn't ready to believe it yet.

Joe pointed a finger at me as he prepared his next question. "When was the last time that you really felt like yourself? When was the last time you felt like the Marcos who helps kids with art, instead of fighting over ideas?"

It had been a while. When Joe called out my desire to do ad work for the lie that it was, I felt like he had pulled at the loose end of a weave that would unravel other lies woven there. I suddenly felt very naked.

"And if it's the money you're worried about, don't give it another negative thought. These things have a way of working themselves out. Leap first, fly later."

"I think we've done enough for today, Marcos," Joe continued. "You have plenty to think about and you have a writing assignment! I can't wait to see what you put out there."

After I left Joe's apartment, all I wanted was to see my kids. I knew Lilly would be at her friend's house and I was relieved when I found Elliott sitting on the couch hunched over an array of gouache paint colors and scattered pages covering the large coffee table in front of him. When I walked in, he slammed his sketchbook closed, sending colored brushes flying. He looked up at me, grabbed his cup of tea, and sank into a recess in the couch.

"Well, I suck," Elliott declared as if pronouncing judgment on himself.

"You don't suck," I said, recalling the lessons from Joe still fresh in my mind.

"Well, I suck at painting. At least tonight I do," he said, unable to look at his closed sketchbook and unwilling to look at me.

I knew this one. It's the stage when art just doesn't work—and the more you try, the worse it gets. I have entire sketchbooks of drawings that I love, but the few ugly ones always want to stand up as proof that my talent was just a transient fluke and that I should quit altogether.

"Don't beat yourself up. And be careful about the words you use to describe yourself."

Did that sound too preachy? I wondered as I sat down next to him. *Elliott's negative tonight. Positive beats negative. Find a compliment as the first step.*

I walked over and sat down next to him. "Can I see what you are working on? Maybe I can get you unstuck?"

Elliott turned to look at me. "Dad, don't. I don't need your help," he barked, but then stopped and changed his tone. "I'm sorry. I'm just frustrated. Art is the one thing that I do . . . the one thing that I'm good at. But I can't exactly call myself an artist if I keep filling these expensive art books with dog crap."

"There, that's the key. You just said it!"

Elliott just looked at me. "What? Dog crap?"

I laughed, but he didn't join me. "No, the thing you are good at. You are good at art and you *know* it." I reached out and grabbed his closed book and handed it to him. "Look, you know what's not working—but take a look and find three things that you like about what you were just working on."

He opened the sketchbook. "It's trash, but I guess the composition is good. I like the underdrawing. And I don't know, the guy's face is okay." He leaned over and held the page open for me.

I looked down at a gray pencil-drawn outline of a man seated at a desk. Messy spots of paint overflowed sections of the chair and the background wall, but the anatomical detail in the seated figure's hands drew me in. I was proud of him and surprised by the quality of parts of the work. "Dude, his hands are amazing."

Elliott's firm face cracked into a smile. "Yeah, hands and feet are my jam."

"Wait here," I said, getting up to retrieve some art supplies from my desk. "Here's some tracing paper. Just lift the under-drawing and then transfer it to the next page. Elliott, this piece is worth saving and working on. After you have the tracing, you can paint another one and another until you get what you want. Burn through as many art supplies as it takes and embrace the beautiful mistakes along the way."

"But aren't we worried about how much these art books cost?"

"We're doing okay. These things have a way of working themselves out, Elliott."

"Can you stay and draw with me for a while?" he asked. "Or do you have to go out and drive tonight?"

"I'm staying in tonight. Give me a pencil, but *you* have to trace the hands."

"Deal."

I drew with him for an hour until the tracing was complete and he was half done transferring it to a fresh page. "I think you've got it from here."

"You're leaving?"

135

"No, I'm just going to get the computer. I have a little art project of my own."

"What is it?" Elliott asked as he went back to his drawing.

"I'm writing down some thoughts and impressions about Joe. I'm going to post it later tonight."

"Is that the old guy that you are caring for?"

"Yes, his name is Joe," I said, opening a new document and stared at the page. "But lately it feels more like he is caring for me."

CHAPTER 9

"You're acting weird," Lilly said to me from the round kitchen table as she watched me nervously prepare the first pot of the day.

"Weird?" I replied. "Weird how?"

"You added coffee to the maker three times. I can feel my hair starting to grow from here and I haven't had a sip yet. Something's up—what is it?"

"I have a job interview this morning," I blurted out. "Well, two actually."

"Dad, that's great," Lilly said, dropping the cynicism from her voice.

"They're just phone interviews, but they are from places that have seen parts of my portfolio—so they know what they would be getting, and they still want to talk to me about a job," I said with a laugh.

"Come on now, your work is good. When are they?"

"Both of them are this morning, kiddo. I guess I am a bit nervous," I said as I poured two strong cups and sat at the table next to her. "It just seems crazy that I have been searching for all this time and now, boom, I get two on the same day. I have to leave for Joe's right after the second one."

I instantly remembered sitting in the car with Joe and asking for this to happen. *Was two in a day because I had asked for it? Could it be that easy?*

"Are you prepared?" Lilly prompted me out of my thoughts.

"Yes, I am," I said, hoping it was true. "The interviews are with two separate universities. I reviewed their recent artwork and the styles they tend to use. They're different from each other, but I think I have figured out how to help them."

I thought back to Joe's lesson on positivity and language. "I *know* I can help them out. I have some ideas that will really work for them."

Lilly turned and tilted her head at me. "Hey, that sounded pretty close to confident," she said with a charming smirk before taking the first sip. "You'll do great, Dad."

"Thanks, Lilly," I said, reaching over to touch her shoulder.

"And you will certainly have enough energy after a cup of this rocket fuel."

I felt a full inch taller as I walked down toward Joe's apartment door. I couldn't wait to tell him how well both interviews had gone. Letting myself in, I heard Joe's voice on the phone talking a bit louder than normal.

"Yes, and be sure to pick up my latest book, *How to Speak for Fun and Profit*, and join my mailing list for updates on events."

I walked in to see him holding a landline telephone receiver to his ear. Joe smiled at me but remained engaged in his conversation while I started on his tea.

"I am teaching a public speaking class this Saturday. It's sponsored by the Colorado Speakers Association and we're affiliated with the National Speakers Association. We teach you everything you need to start your public speaking career: how to find and refine your topics, how to practice, how to find your first venue, and we even teach you how to build your audience with public relations like getting on the radio."

"Ha! You see, I got on your station and that's proof that the system works. You can register online and there are still a few spots available. I hope to see everyone there, and remember— speakers speak!"

Joe reached over to hang up the phone and look up at me.

"Wow, Joe," I started. "What was that?"

"I was on a local radio show that hosts me sometimes. I'm drumming up business for my next class—*our* next class," he added.

Almost ninety and still on radio shows drumming up business? I thought to myself. *Half his body has broken down, but he just keeps going. Most people are retired by sixty-five and dead before eighty.* "Why do you do it, Joe?"

"I just told you. I'm getting the word out there through my media connections. It's the same process and steps to get media coverage that I teach in the course. You'll see."

"No, Joe. Why are you still doing this? Why are you working so hard at your age? Don't you think you should take it easy?"

"Nonsense," Joe retorted. "I love it. Do what you love and you'll never work a day in your life. I haven't worked a day in over fifty-five years. Besides, the older the better I say. Are any of us too old to follow our dreams?"

"I suppose you're right." *Maybe I wasn't too old to follow my dream of going to grad school at fifty-one.* "I just thought . . ."

"Marcos, I've lived a long life, long enough to know what I enjoy—and I enjoy this work. If you keep helping me get around, I will get to continue helping people reach their potential."

"Sounds like a good plan," I said, eager to move away from the topic of age. "What else do you need to do to prepare for the class?"

"I'm set. I've got everything standardized so it's very straight-forward. I hope you can still help me run it as we talked about."

"I got you, Joe. I'm excited about it."

"Wow! I can't wait until Saturday to do it with you."

"I have some other exciting news, Joe," I said as I pulled over his computer chair and sat down. "I just had two interviews this morning."

"Two? Which two? The universities?"

"Yes, it was with both of the schools."

"And?" Joe said, his infectious enthusiasm transforming him into a curious boy.

"And it went great," I answered. It felt good to say it out loud to someone. "Both of them were great."

"Tell me all about it," Joe said as he blew at the steam rising from his cup.

"They both sent me nice emails asking to talk to me right away. Coronado College was first. Joe, I did exactly what we practiced. I piqued their interest by complimenting their work and offered ideas on how I knew I could expand on it. I built that desire you talked about by showing them what they will gain with my experience in surveys and persona branding. And I closed it by telling them how I would improve their job flow, make their branding consistent across all channels, and reach more students with retargeting ads. I kept everything positive and the whole interview just flowed so well. Before I knew it, we were done and they want me to come on campus and interview with them in person."

"Wow! That's fantastic. I knew you could do it. You're going to knock their socks off."

"And then I had a phone interview with Naropa right before I came over this morning. Joe, everything you prepared me for worked perfectly there too. I told them I was very excited about their art therapy program and the interviewer told me that she was taking classes on the tuition reimbursement benefit too. We really hit it off."

"That's amazing, Marcos. How did each interview feel to you?"

"I liked both of the people I interviewed with and both schools seem good. Coronado asked me a few questions about my faith. I was worried at first. I was raised as a Christian but for the last ten years or so, my relationship with God has been less about going to church and more about listening for spiritual guidance. I answered honestly and the man interviewing me seemed to like my answer. I could see myself working there and getting along.

"The Naropa interview felt a bit better now that I think about it, Joe. They asked a question that seemed tough at first. But when I answered it, it made the Buddhist school feel more welcoming."

"What did they ask you?"

"They asked, as a graphic design director at Naropa, how would I contribute to diversity and inclusion to transform student life on campus? Joe, we did *not* prepare for that question. But I thought about Elliott attending the school and then I just imagined how I could make him feel at home. My answers came pretty easily and they must have worked because they are checking their calendar for when they want to bring me on campus for an interview with their management team."

"Marcos, that's two for two. I'm so proud of you," Joe said, beaming. "You did really well."

"Is this because I asked for it in the car with you?"

Joe smiled and looked over at me. "What do you think?"

I knew he was going to ask me that, I thought. *Just as I knew that I was the only one who could answer it.* Six months of searching with not even a callback or follow-up questionnaire and now two interviews in one day. It was hard to come to any other conclusion than Joe's guidance to ask for it out loud had worked. *If that were true, what else should I be asking for?*

"Well, it feels like more than just coincidence to me, Joe," I conceded. "What other tricks do you have in that bag of yours?"

"Ha! We're just getting started on you. Let's talk about it over lunch. We have a special guest joining us today. My ex-wife Judy will be joining us, at least for the beginning."

"Your ex-wife?" I asked in surprise. I'd never thought to ask him about anything personal like this. "You're divorced?"

"Yep, but it was amicable and we're still very close and special to one another. We're just better off not being married to each other. She's my best friend."

"I look forward to meeting her," I said, but kept wondering what could have broken up his marriage.

"Oh, she'll love you. She likes to chat with my caregivers, especially when they're men. Let's get my pin on and get going."

Leading Joe through the front doors of Perkins, I looked up to see a short, older woman with short-cropped white hair sitting in Joe's usual booth. She saw me walking with Joe at the same time and gave me a wide smile before standing up to greet us.

"Judy, my dear, how are you?" Joe said, shuffling forward to hug her. "This is my new caregiver, Marcos Perez."

"Nice to meet you, Marcos," Judy said, extending a small hand.

They were about the same height and looked like they would have been a perfect couple.

"Let's sit down and have some lunch. I wonder which server we'll get today," Joe said, looking around.

"I already ordered a sandwich, Joe. I have an appointment so I will need to leave early. How long have you been looking after our Joe?" Judy asked me.

I tried to remember my start date. "About three months."

"That's wonderful. Have you provided care for others before?"

"No, it is my first time doing anything like this," I replied.

"But he's a natural," Joe interjected. "He was a dance teacher so when he leads me around I feel as light on my feet as Fred Astaire."

"I hate to break it to you, but I think you're Ginger in this duet," Judy joked.

"I guess you're right," Joe conceded. "He's an artist too. He just completed not one but two interviews for artist jobs this morning."

"Is that your normal work?"

"It is," I replied. "I'm a graphic designer, but I've been unemployed for nine months now."

Twyla, Joe's favorite server, brought out a sandwich and a glass of tea for Judy before taking our usual order.

"Do you have any kids, Marcos?" Judy asked before starting her lunch.

"I have two kids," I answered before thinking about the follow-up. "A girl and a boy."

"Are you married, Marcos?"

"You'll have to forgive all the questions," Joe interrupted. "Judy asks a lot of questions. She's a public speaker and a life coach and her coaching method is about asking questions."

And yours isn't? I said to myself as I remembered his deep questions like *why are you here?* and *when is the last time you really felt like yourself?* "I'm divorced, two years now."

"Well, that's three of us," Judy said. "And it's not the end of the world. Sometimes it's just what we need to grow in new ways."

"I feel like we've both grown since our divorce," Joe said in agreement, but I sensed a touch of something like sadness in his words compared to Judy's.

"I've grown in ways I couldn't have imagined," Judy added. "I coach people that it's important to ask yourself what lessons you learned from a major event like a divorce, otherwise everything can just feel like loss."

"I learned that sometimes you need to let people go if that's what they want," I said in what felt like a confession.

"That sounds like a valuable lesson, Marcos," Joe chimed in.

"But maybe not an easy one," Judy replied as though she were saying the words for me.

I just nodded and looked around for our server to see if I could get Joe's coffee prepared and change the topic to something else. Joe and Judy caught up on things and I got the feeling that they did this lunch a few times a year. I also learned that Judy was Joe's backup plan if his caregiver couldn't assist with running his courses.

"Marcos has agreed to help me run my next course," Joe said with pride, reaching over and patting my arm as our plates arrived.

"Good," Judy said, looking at us both. "I'm sure you two will be quite a pair. I should be going, Joe. Marcos, it was a pleasure, and thanks for taking care of my Joe."

I moved over to the other side of the booth after Judy left and I just said the first thing on my mind. "Joe, I have a hard time imagining why you two would split up."

He took a sip of his coffee as he thought about his answer. "Lots of people have asked me that, especially people in the Colorado Speakers Association. We founded it together, you know. She said she wanted us to grow in new ways, but I think we had just helped each other as much as we could and that we needed something more than either of us was able to offer."

I dug into my free lunch and thought about his answer. *Had Ursula wanted more than I was able to offer?*

"I don't view our marriage ending as a failure, but I do miss her. She's my best friend. I still love her very much."

"It shows."

Joe smiled and then looked up at me. "You shouldn't view your divorce as a failure either."

I nodded, but I couldn't agree with his suggestion. "I tried my best to be a good husband and it blew up in my face. I couldn't help but feel like a failure—both to her and to my kids."

"That failure you're still feeling might be more about the role you were playing than about you," Joe said, narrowing in on me.

"Role? What role? You mean as a husband?"

"You didn't say husband," Joe countered. "You said *good* husband. Judy has a great technique in her coaching. She calls it asking the questions you're not asking. I love that. The question you're not asking is, was it more important to your wife for you to be a good husband or to continue being a good Marcos?"

That *was* a question I hadn't been asking myself and it seared my ears to hear it potentially two years too late.

"You're not alone, Marcos. Many people make this mistake. You see, your wife was attracted to the good Marcos—the artist, the dancer, the musician. But sometimes we get lost in the roles we think we need to play and those roles, like father or husband or friend or employee, can become comfortable places for us to hide in. Do you think she got what she wanted in the exchange?"

"No," I answered instinctively while I thought back to how I was feeling about myself before our marriage ended. *Some spark had gone out in me, and I had faded into some provider or husband or dad role that was less than what I should have been.*

"Don't hide, Marcos. Don't ever hide. Be your true self, even if you have to rediscover it."

Even after three, going on four, months of being with him, I was still blown away by the wisdom that could pour out of this man at any moment. "You're right, Joe. I know you're right because that is pretty much what happened the night our relationship ended."

"Do you feel like talking about it?"

I looked out the window to gather my thoughts and rein in my racing emotions. *Why is this failure still so fresh for me?* "I've never told anyone this story before. Not even my kids."

"I'm listening."

"We had been going sideways for a while. I had been working hard, too hard, at my job, putting in overtime taking on extra projects to bring in more money. She grew more distant from me during the times that I was home. By the time I'd noticed the gap between us and started reaching out to suggest things for us to do together, it was too late. It was like I was losing myself and my identity trying to chase after her. It worked for a while, but she was already gone."

I stopped talking for a moment as I recalled the events that brought me to the end. Joe just sat and listened.

"I wanted to do something special for her, so I got tickets to her favorite band and invited our closest friends—like a double date. It was great. She seemed so happy, and I was too. But after the show started, she just ditched me and ran toward the stage and started dancing in a crowd of strangers. I waited for a song, and then another, and another after that. And when she didn't come back and didn't seem to have any intention to, I was just like, *what will it take to connect with this woman?* I felt frustrated and after a while, I went down toward the stage to see what was up. When I got down there, she was dancing but there were these two guys dancing with her, and they were all over her.

"And Joe, like a good husband, I grab the guy closest to her and yell at him, 'Hey, that's my wife.' And that must have been the wrong thing to do because she got so upset with me for pulling them off. I couldn't believe what was happening and I just lost it and said to myself, *I can't be here right now.*"

"So what did you do?" Joe asked.

"I just left the concert and started walking home. It's the only thing I could think to do at the time."

"Was it far?"

I laughed out loud. "Yes, it was. I marked it off with the car a few days later. Joe, it was fifteen miles."

"Fifteen miles? What were you thinking?"

"I wasn't thinking, I was just reacting. But the interesting thing is I *kept* reacting. I remember being so mad. I was furious as I walked. I was walking along a road and shouting my anger up at the night sky, but by the time I was just starting to get over my rage, I still had nine miles more to go. It was like two in the morning at that point and I had two to three hours more before I would get home. Weeping came after the anger. I just felt so sad as I walked and thought about my life without her and what would happen to the kids. So there I was, walking and blubbering along the side of the highway like some lunatic. I was out of emotions after the ten-mile mark, and I just felt like I was empty of all the feelings that were making me try for her so hard. And then it was just me, walking alone on the side of a highway. I remember the night was perfect—warm temperature, clear with a million stars overhead—and as I walked, I looked up at the stars, feeling nothing, and I sort of reconnected with myself and realized that I had wandered so far away from the real me while I had been chasing her. Everything felt so light after that, because I was free from all those emotions holding me down from chasing something that was already gone. Then it was just me."

"The real Marcos," Joe emphasized.

149

"Yes, and at that moment I realized that I had been missing myself and I wanted to keep that lightness. And that's the exact moment that I knew it was over."

"I think you learned a valuable lesson. No," Joe corrected, "a precious lesson."

I nodded. "That wasn't the only lesson I learned that night. It was about ten minutes after this beautiful revelation that the police car rolled up behind me with its lights flashing. Apparently, it's illegal to walk along a highway, who knew? The officer told me there had been reports of a madman crying and screaming at the sky as he walked next to the highway."

Joe couldn't control his laughter. "I can just picture it. What a scene," he said as I started laughing along with him.

It felt good to tell the story and it *did* have a funny ending. "They commiserated with what had happened and decided to give me a ride home. But when you ride in a police car, they have to handcuff you for safety reasons. So there I was, emotionally spent, completely exhausted, and then handcuffed before they placed me into the back seat of their car. People were honking and shouting out the window at me and all three of us just started laughing at what a bad night I was having."

"Oh god," Joe laughed out loud as people started to look over at us. "Stop it."

"They gave me a ride home and I walked in right before sunrise. She was awake and was worried about me. I just stood in the doorway looking at her and said, 'I'm done.' And that was it."

"You stopped hiding."

"Yes, I did," I said. "You asked me a question a few days ago that has been running through my head ever since. 'When is the last time I really felt like myself?' I think that time walking on the highway alone under those stars was the last time. I feel like every day since then, I have drifted a little farther from how pure I felt on that night."

"Well, it sounds like you know where your spot on the map is. We just need to keep working toward getting you back there."

"Things are turning around for me since I met you," I said. "I thought the caregiver ad said I was supposed to be helping you, Joe."

"Well, you wouldn't have answered the ad if it was worded the other way around," he answered with a sly smile as he picked up the check again.

I felt the phone buzz in my pocket, and I looked down to see a text from the ad firm asking me if I could do an in-person interview at 3:00 p.m. "Joe, you're not going to believe this, but the ad agency just texted me; they want to speak to me in two hours."

"Another interview? Wow, that's amazing, Marcos. We should get going so you can be ready, but before we do—can we talk about what you wrote?"

"Wrote? I didn't prepare anything for the interviews."

"Not that. You were going to write something about yourself and our time together. I looked online and I didn't see anything," Joe said with a touch of disappointment and a sidelong glance. "I was beginning to think you didn't write it, but that can't be true—can it?"

"Oh, that. I have it, Joe. I didn't post it because I wanted you to see it first. I have it on my laptop in the bag here," I said, reaching for the computer. "Do you want to see it?"

Joe brightened at the news that I had completed his assignment. "Yes, I want to see your assignment."

I started my tired and scuffed laptop and opened the document file I had written about our time together. But when I opened the file only the first two sentences appeared on the page. A sinking feeling washed over me as I looked in my directories for other copies or backups. *Did I forget to save it?*

"What's the matter?" Joe asked.

"I can't find the complete document now. I just have the first two sentences, but I wrote almost two pages. I must not have saved it," I confessed. *What a dullard*, I said to myself as I continued my frantic search.

"You didn't write it," Joe stated, clearly disappointed.

"I did, Joe," I defended. "It didn't save, or the file got corrupted somehow, but I *did* write it."

"I really hoped that you would do the work, Marcos," Joe said flatly as he started scooching toward the opening of the booth as an indicator that he was ready to leave.

"I'll find it, Joe. That or I'll write it again."

He stopped moving and looked up at me. "You're not going to write it. I'm ready to go, Marcos. And you need to prepare for your next interview."

I helped him to his feet and started toward the door, but the bubble of positivity that normally surrounded Joe had burst. I held his hand and replayed his reaction in my mind. *Was he that disappointed in me? Was this really a failure—if I did write it, but didn't save it? Was he starting to pull back because he knew that I would get one of these jobs and might soon be gone? Was it some melancholy about seeing his ex-wife?* I had no idea what had changed his mood so quickly, but his disappointment felt like a spell had been broken and I wanted more than anything to get it back.

I spent the first hour after dinner trying to find and recover the missing section of the file, but it was gone. The second hour I spent trying to rewrite it so I could show it to Joe in the morning. But, after the less-than-optimal interview with the ad agency, I just kept coming back to the feeling of disappointment from him as we left Perkins. Joe's words, "You're not going to write it," rang in my ears, half indictment, half prediction. *Joe had a habit of being right about these things.*

I closed the laptop and pulled up the Uber app to look for rides that could start my night toward something productive. I was just in time for the after-dinner rush and the first passenger of the night was Brett.

Fortyish and built like an athlete, he jumped in the car and was very jovial and friendly. Normally, I love these riders, but I was still feeling off from how things had ended with Joe in the afternoon. After the first mile of chatting with me, he leaned forward from the back seat. "Sorry, man, I don't mean to talk your ears off."

I laughed. "No, it's okay. I love passengers like you. I was just thinking about my day. It started strong, but really fell off a cliff at the end. Have you ever disappointed someone important to you?"

He laughed out loud. "Dude, I'm married—so that's like every day."

I smiled as we pulled onto the highway and his energy changed as he slid back in the seat. "Do you have kids?" he asked. "Like high school?"

I nodded.

"Complete asses, right?"

I hadn't expected that, and it cracked me up. "Some days."

"I'm kidding. We love them, right? That's why I'm out slinging medical equipment and having dinner away from them. And that's why you're out driving drunks home from the bar."

"Yep," I said, taking a full inventory of his assessment.

"That used to be me," Brett said, looking at the cars next to us as we drove. "I'm sober two years now. So yeah, I have disappointed some people who are important to me."

"What did you do to fix it?" I asked as I kept my eyes on the road ahead.

"I'm still working on that part. Did you disappoint someone?"

"I did," I said, remembering the change in feelings from Joe at the end of the day. "It didn't seem like a big deal to me, but I could tell that something was different after he thought I failed to do what I said I would do."

"I know it can feel like an overreaction, but their feelings are valid. AA showed me I had been focusing only on myself and I had been ignoring the love and investment that others were making in me for the change that I needed."

"What did you do?"

"Respect their feelings and point of view as a start. Then look for how they were trying to help and recognize that. In the twelve-step program they talk about making amends. It sure looks easy when you read that step on a poster. The hard part is getting the chance to do it. Think about making amends now, so that you'll be ready when the opportunity comes."

CHAPTER 10

Driving to Joe's apartment on the Saturday of the class, my mind felt like it was caught in a loop of replaying his disappointment after lunch, my disastrous interview in the afternoon, and Brett's advice on making amends last night. *Had Joe overreacted or was he frustrated that I wasn't making the progress he expected?* I considered both and realized it didn't matter. What *did* matter was making it right and trying to get everything back to normal between us. *Let positive beat negative.*

Closing the door behind me, I heard rustling papers in the living room. "Good morning, Joe."

"Marcos, you're just in time. Can you come here and help me organize these student packets?"

Stacks of blue, green, yellow, and red papers lay on the couch cushions and armrests next to scattered blank CDs. "What's all this?"

"It's the student materials. I meant to organize this last night, but I pooped out," Joe confessed. "There is a number and a title for each page, please collate them into order and put a CD with each one."

I followed his instructions, and he sat back down on the couch. *CDs?* I thought as I placed a disc in each bifold packet.

I need to get him some USB drives. "How many students are you expecting?"

"We have eight who have registered and six who have pre-paid. Let's prepare twelve just to be safe. Sometimes they bring others at the last minute. We have a room in the back at Perkins for the class. We should leave soon to set everything up."

I prepared the twelve packets and packed a few extra Almond Joys and Ensure drinks to keep him going. "Joe, I want to talk about yesterday," I said, deciding to make my opportunity instead of waiting.

"Yes," Joe replied.

"I'm sorry I disappointed you. I should have just posted what I wrote about us like you asked me to do. I can tell that you really care, and I appreciate the help, Joe."

"Well, Marcos, I'm glad you appreciate it," Joe started as he leaned back into the comfy brown couch. "There are two types of people that I work with—those who do, and those who don't. What I offer each of them is the same, but the resulting joy, fulfillment, and happiness I hope to see in their lives always boils down to whether they do the work or not."

"I understand." I sat on the office chair in front of the computer and took in his words.

"Marcos, you could be giving ukulele lessons right now if you wanted to—but you didn't. You said you would post something—but you didn't. So when you tell me that you want to use your artistic ability to help others, I see how high the stakes are—not just for you, but for countless people who you will help long after I'm gone," he said as he looked down at his contrasting hands. "This is important, Marcos. What we're doing together is important. Be a doer. Take action. Make a difference in other people's lives."

He was right—again. I thought back to every lesson he tried to teach me, every positive example he provided, every thumb in the back prompt to do the next good thing. *What did he see in me that was so special? Is inaction just another form of hiding? Could I be doing so much more?* "You're right, Joe. I'll be a doer."

"Our language has so much power, Marcos," Joe said, brightening into a wide smile. "I want you to say that again but put it into present tense this time." He raised his right hand twice as a cue.

"I'm a doer."

"How does that feel?" he asked, his blinking eyes popping with excitement behind the think lenses.

It *did* feel different. "I'm a doer," I repeated. *I believed it.* "It feels right, Joe."

Joe smiled and nodded.

"Well, one thing that I said I would do is to help you run this course today," I stated. "I think we should get to it."

"That's the spirit! Pack up everything and let's go."

Joe looked over at me as I drove us to Perkins. "I forgot to ask you, Mr. Three Interviews in One Day—how did the final one go?"

"Ugh," I groaned. "Not good."

"Oh no."

"No, that's not quite right. It was a disaster."

"What happened?"

"I'm still replaying it in my head—the whole thing was a nightmare really," I confessed and already felt better for being able to share it with someone. "The moment I walked into the stainless steel and frosted glass reception area, I could tell it was a miss. The woman at the front desk was cooler than I will ever be—Betty Page haircut, retro tattoos, and designer glasses. Every agency has one of these; they set the standard for cool as soon as you walk in. And then I walk in looking like a narc in my sport coat and slacks. She looked at me like I was lost, before eventually sending me in to see the creative director."

"What was he like?"

"He was one of those outdoor adventure dads that just stepped out of a 'Vacation in Colorado' poster. He had even more tattoos under rolled-up flannel sleeves and a long hipster beard. The director led me back into a conference room to meet their senior copywriter. She was the nice one—at first. They told me they were looking for help with a national electric bike client and I saw an opportunity to start the interview with a compliment like I had done with the other two. So I mentioned that I love e-bikes and complimented them for working in such a cool and emerging sector. They liked that I had worked with big brand names like Ford and The Metropolitan Opera. When I opened my book, Mr. Flannel said, 'Oh, you brought an actual portfolio, old-school.' I walked them through the creative strategy for each piece and they didn't say much. When I was on my fourth example, the creative director interrupted. 'Well, I am going to be honest with you. With these great logos, I thought the creative would have been stronger.' Then the copywriter lady chimed in, 'We're not saying it's bad, I am just not a fan of cutesy illustration work. Maybe you should be a children's book illustrator.' I knew she meant well, but that really stung. I wanted to climb between the pages of my old-school portfolio and just close the book on myself."

"Oh, come on now," Joe interjected. "It couldn't have been that bad. Was that the end of the interview?"

"Oh no," I continued. "They wanted to see more. It was like I was looking at my work through their eyes as they picked apart every decision. 'Your model looks like a soccer mom.' 'Well, this company's campaign used actual employees with real customer success stories,' I answered. 'You can tell that is a stock image.' 'We used the budget savings for ad spend,' I defended."

Joe did an amazing job of just looking at me and listening with his full attention.

"I just closed my book when the creative director looked down at his phone. 'I don't mean to be rude, but it's just not a fit for us,' he said. 'Can I give you some advice? With this level of work, you might be a better fit for agencies that service local, smaller clients.' I pretended this advice was not an insult and I thanked them for bringing me in—and that was the end of the interview."

"Marcos, when someone says no, just let them go."

"That's easy for you to say. From what I've seen, no one tells you no."

"That's not true," Joe protested. "Earlier this week, you walked in while I was on the radio. Do you know how many 'no thank you' answers I had to get to that one yes?"

I hadn't considered how hard he might still have to work to get PR for his classes.

"In my class today, you'll see that it takes hundreds of out-reaches to get one or two yeses that are a good fit."

"Yes, but their criticism was so brutal. I felt crushed as I walked out."

"Marcos, do you like your work?"

I really didn't after the interview. "Well, I did before I walked in there."

Joe shook his head at me. "What is the name of the agency?"

"Bramble Fire."

Joe raised his right hand and then motioned for me to do the same thing. "Say, 'Bye-bye, Bramble Fire.'" He smiled and waved.

I waved too. "Bye, Bramble Fire—jerks," I said with a laugh.

"That's it," Joe chuckled. "Shake off those nos and keep going. You got two out of three yesterday, Marcos. I'd take that any day."

I said a few more internal goodbyes to my hopes of working there, but I couldn't let it go. "I felt like I could have taken my graphics game to a new level with them. They are the best."

"No," Joe interjected. "They would have taken everything you love about yourself and your art and turned it into a cheap copy of themselves."

Well, probably expensive copies, but Joe is right—yet again, I thought as I pulled into the restaurant parking lot.

"Why would you sell the best of yourself so cheap?" Joe asked. "It's a long life, but it's over quickly. Doing work that you are not passionate about is like prostituting yourself. Don't do that. Wait for the right fit, Marcos."

"You're right. Thanks for talking me through this. I'm sorry for dropping all this negativity on you before you start your course."

"Ha, do you think that small drama could unsettle me?" Joe scoffed. "It's going to be amazing today, Marcos. Are you ready?"

We arrived and I set up the folding tables and chairs they had placed in the private back room for us. "What do you want me to do?" I asked.

"Just follow my lead. As I go through the class, I will ask you to distribute the printouts. You'll see, I have a system."

The room was carpeted and decorated in Perkins greens and tans, but without any booths or windows. I greeted the students and Joe spoke with each one as they arrived until we had six. Joe kicked things off by asking each person to stand up and explain why they had signed up and what they wanted to achieve through the class.

First was a returning middle-aged couple who had taken his course last year and now had written a book that they wanted to promote. Next was a thirtyish woman who was taking the course as part of a professional advancement track at a software firm. She was followed by a newly retired man who wanted to make money talking about fly-fishing, and the last two were a father and young daughter team who had been attending Toastmasters meetings and wanted to take the course after hearing about it there. The daughter wanted more speaking practice before her presentation at the science fair, and Dad wanted to be a better presenter in company meetings.

I could feel hints of doubt from some of them as they eyed old Joe and then me at the front of the room, wondering who the speaker was, who was the assistant, and what they had signed up for.

After the last person sat back down, Joe chimed in. "All of you just did a brave thing. You stood up and spoke about yourself in front of strangers. Congratulations! That makes you a public speaker. How did it feel to do that?"

All six students murmured a few thoughts until nine-year-old Madison stood up again. "It made me feel powerful that everyone was listening to what I was saying. It made me want to do a good job."

"That's a very common feeling," Joe said to her before lifting his eyes to the others. "It feels different to say it out loud, doesn't it? This is because you are not just talking anymore, but actively trying to hold other people's attention with your words as you deliver an important message—it's different when speaking publicly."

162

Joe stopped to take a drink of water and then turned to me. "Marcos, can you hand out the blue worksheets to everyone?"

I took the blue pages from the multicolored stack and handed them out.

"The two primary drivers to speaking successfully are passion and engagement," Joe stated. "I believe everyone is here on this earth for a reason. We need to find that reason and then contribute our unique gift to others. The words we use as public speakers have the power to change people's lives. I have changed lives through my words, and I have trained thousands of speakers over the past fifty years to do the same thing."

I started to feel nervous for Joe as the father looked at his watch and the software engineer was fidgeting in her chair.

"But don't confuse speaking with contributing," Joe continued. "You will learn how to be a public speaker today, but I want to challenge each of you to take what you learn here and think about how you can share your passion, your reason for being here, to other people."

Everyone in the group, including me, nodded in agreement.

"I spoke with each of you, and I learned that some of you already know your calling, or as I like to call it—the song you came here to sing. Some of you might still be searching for it—and that's okay."

Joe smiled and looked each person in the eye. "Thank you for accepting my challenge; now let's talk about engagement. Have you ever heard someone speak who just goes on and on and never gets to his point?"

Several people nodded.

"This is a lack of consideration for the audience, and it is the most common problem that new public speakers face. What did you do when that happened?"

"Well, yawning mostly," Abbie, the software engineer, said.

Joe's eyes lit up. "That's right! That is not the *result* the speaker wanted, and it is not the result you want. To overcome this, we as public speakers need a formula for a 'results-getting talk.'"

I looked down at the blue sheet in my hand and read the title: "Results-Getting Talk." Joe was right on track.

"The first step of that formula is to find the problem that you came here to solve, then find the pain. Only then should you think about offering a solution. And lastly, get your audience to take action. Action is key, because if there is no action then you are just entertaining them. And we are here to make a difference, a contribution. Speaking is a gift and having an audience is an honor."

Laura, the woman with the new book, raised her hand. "Richard and I just finished a book on camping in Colorado. Camping really isn't a problem and there's no pain involved. Do you know what I'm saying? It's just what we love doing."

Joe took a moment, and I looked over to see if her question might sidetrack him.

"Well, if you want to camp but you don't know where the best spots are, then that is a problem," Joe added.

Richard spoke up with some doubt clouding his statement. "But our book isn't a how-to guide—it's about inspiring people to get out there and enjoy Colorado."

"Oh, that's even better," Joe countered with a bright smile as he spoke up for the whole room. "Go about halfway down on the blue page and underline the phrase 'Find the Hurt.' This is skipping ahead a bit, but Richard has provided a great example of getting to the 'why' of what you are speaking about."

Joe turned back to Laura and Richard. "Why do you camp?"

I smiled and chuckled inside as I flashed back to a confused me on Joe's brown couch struggling through a similar question. *Did Joe have these people right where he wanted them?* I wondered.

Richard took a moment to answer. "After a week of stressing out over every little email, or hiring decision, or office politics, I just want to get away! When we are driving up into the mountains, it feels like we're escaping to a life that's simpler."

Laura chimed in. "I feel human again, even for just a weekend. That's all it takes to heal my heart from the modern world."

"That's great," Joe said to each of them. "Now try restating that as a problem."

Richard looked up as he thought about Joe's challenge. "I guess the real problem is that people are disconnected from nature."

"That's pretty good," Joe acknowledged. "Try restating it again, but this time as a problem that only your book can solve."

"People are disconnected from *their* nature," Laura added with a satisfied smile, now getting into the exercise.

"Now you have it." Joe leaned forward in his chair as if to drive his point home with them. "Can you see your unique contribution here? Write down what you are here to solve for others."

I reached for my journal and started writing as I watched Joe work his magic with Laura and Richard. The fly fisherman and the father started actively taking notes.

"We connect people to nature so they can reconnect with themselves," Richard declared along with Laura's nodding approval.

"How does that feel?"

"That feels like purpose," Laura said.

"That feels amazing," Richard added with confidence. "It's like I can't wait to tell people about it."

"Great!" Joe encouraged. "Now what action do you want them to take?"

Richard laughed. "Get your butts out there into nature!"

Joe smiled and chuckled along with them. "Do you see a title for your talk forming?"

Joe leaned over to me and whispered for me to distribute the green worksheet. "We're ready for 'How to Create a Title that Sizzles and Sells.' Go to the top of the page on the new sheet and think about a benefit or two. What are your audience, or your readers, going to get after they take action?"

"We have connecting with yourself and connecting with nature," Laura continued.

"That's good," Joe urged. "Write that down, then add the action to it."

Richard raised a finger and laughed. "Why don't we just go with 'Get Out There'?"

Joe made a fist with his right hand and drew it closer to his clenched left one in cue to bring the phrases together.

"'Get Out There,'" Laura prompted, "'and Connect with Yourself . . . and Nature.'"

Abbie the software designer suddenly shot up her arm like a kid in a classroom. "I've got it. 'Get Out There and *Find* Yourself in Nature.'"

Everyone in the room erupted in agreement and wanted to talk about their subject next.

Laura grinned and playfully punched her husband in the shoulder. "Now we'll have to change the title of the book!"

I looked up from the notes I was capturing in the journal just in time to see Joe at the perfect moment. The small man next to me wasn't a broken old man anymore. The collected years fell off him and he stood radiant and glorious, basking in the collective enthusiasm of his audience as they continued to bounce creative ideas off one another. I had just watched Joe manifest this great idea out of nothing, just like a magician, in the back room of Perkins. *This is the next good thing*, I thought as I watched him enjoy the breakthrough moment he had created for Laura and Richard. *Has he been doing it like this since the 1970s? Do all his classes energize people this way?* I asked myself as I watched him work his small audience.

Joe had captured us all and it was amazing. We all wanted to help others. We wanted to be speakers and now believed we could. We all wanted to find the problem we were here to solve and share it with others.

In a way, I was relieved that I hadn't posted what I had written and lost about Joe because it would have come too short of this high mark. The next two hours were a download of more magic and motivation under Joe's spell as he revisited everyone's goal from the introductions.

"Wow!" Joe interjected to get control of the room again. "Who's ready to talk about fly-fishing?"

Driving away from the restaurant, I looked over at Joe, who was still glowing from the interactions with his students. "So, Joe," I started. "That was amazing. That is a real talent! I have done naming and rebranding exercises for decades and your method is outstanding. Do you feel like that is your song, Joe?"

"What, that?" Joe countered. "No, that's just something I'm good at. My song is what happens as a result of sharing that talent. Don't confuse talent with calling—sometimes they align, but sometimes the things we're good at can become a comfortable place to hide."

"What do you mean?"

"If you are good at dancing or playing the ukulele or—what did you call it?" Joe asked, struggling to recall my term.

"Naming and rebranding."

"If you are good at art or naming and rebranding, maybe that is your calling or your song—but maybe that talent is a path to something else, something more meaningful. Miss the turn sign for that path and your talent can become a dead end instead of a wonderful journey."

I thought about my art talent, still licking my wounds from Bramble Fire. *Just because you can do something well, does that mean you should? Or should you aim to have an impact?* I was still buzzing from the energy of Joe's course and all I wanted to do was the next good thing. *Had I been making my whole life about what I could do well? Maybe my art talent is a path to something else.* And right on cue, Joe asked the perfect question.

"Why art therapy?"

I drove slower to give myself the time to answer. I didn't have a ready answer to his question, but I knew that if I opened up about it, I would find something there. "I use art to express things, deep subconscious things that hang around in the shadows and jump out at you at the worst possible times."

Joe looked over at me, magnified eyes full of compassion as if he sensed me opening up.

"Sometimes I meditate to calm my mind and sometimes an image comes. When I can see it clearly, I grab my sketchbook and capture it before it moves away from me. The image I draw might not even look like anything recognizable and it may take days of working on it before my conscious mind can understand it. I know it might sound weird and metaphysical," I said, looking over to see if he was still listening, "but it has helped me deal with deep, deep sadness and old traumas. When I think about that, I think there must be artistic kids out there who could heal that same way."

"Do you know any kids who need this kind of artistic healing?" Joe asked.

Dang, I thought to myself as I drove, *how does he always ask the perfect question? How is* he *not a therapist?* "I know one."

"Your son, Elliott?"

I just nodded as I fought to keep my rising emotions in check at the memory of Elliott's struggles through transition and his suicide attempt.

"Do you want to talk about it?"

Again, just the right question. *Because I did want to talk about it. But would he understand?* "You're not supposed to bring up the past after the person transitions. But I have to bring it up to set the context. I mentioned to you before that Elliott wasn't always Elliott."

Joe turned his head to me but didn't ask a question.

"It was at the end of the seventh grade that I started to see something was different. It started with dressing in black, listening to dark music, and hanging out with new friends and I thought, 'Well, this must be the next phase.' But then one day, I hear my kid use a new voice on the playground—it was like a man's voice,

PEREZ AND MAIKRANZ

deep and powerful, and I thought, 'Oh, that's different.' The next year was the start of high school and my oldest just announced to me one day, 'Dad, I think I'm a lesbian.' And I remember thinking, 'Okay, good.' Elliott made new friends in the gay crowd. They were super cool and creative types and I think they were popular. He seemed really happy hanging out with them."

I looked over at Joe, who seemed to be absorbing every word. It felt great to talk to someone about this.

"Elliott's troubles started when his school ran this effort to connect students with each other around their differences. They called it 'Sharing Is Caring' but it was more like 'Naming and Shaming' after what happened. The faculty was trying to get kids to open up about themselves in a 'safe space' environment. Faculty members spoke with selected students one-on-one to help them share. Elliott shared about being gay, but then his counselor encouraged him to come all the way out as transgender. So he talked in the group about how he felt male on the inside and wanted to live that way on the outside. But news of this private 'caring moment' where my kid shared the truth about himself spread through the halls and quickly turned into a feeding frenzy of harassment for every bully who had a problem with it. Elliott spent his days being shoved into walls and they called him every name you can imagine. Even Oliver, one of his friends from the cool gay kids club, was hateful and intolerant to him. 'I may be gay, but trans people don't exist. It's not a real thing. You are an abomination to God,' said his friend.

"Elliott was upset and depressed, but it didn't end with just insults and social media fights. Weeks later, someone snuck up

170

behind him and yelled 'Hey, Tranny' and shoved him down the stairs at school. Elliott was knocked unconscious and was taken to the nurse's office. He didn't mention anything at the time and their bullying was driving him deeper into depression."

"People can be cruel about things they don't understand," Joe said. "And sometimes kids can be the cruelest."

"I think they were, Joe," I said as I fought back the tears that always came when reliving this. "It got worse and worse for him. All the bullying eventually pushed him to the top of the stairs on the third floor of the school. Elliott later told me that he had climbed up onto the metal railing and looked down through the opening in the stair flights to the basement level four floors below. He was going to jump. That was his escape plan. He stood there without hope as he thought about his missing friends, his misunderstood life, and his mistake of a body.

"Can you imagine a fifteen-year-old thinking that no one in the world would ever love him, or accept him, or even treat him fairly? In that moment of imagining day after day of continued suffering, being dead seemed like the best way to solve his problem. The only thing that stopped him from jumping was the thought to call his mother. He called her and climbed down. But even after talking to her, and then to me, he was still determined to kill himself. I still have the image of him, perched on top of that railing—looking down through the opening to the last thing he would ever see."

I exhaled sharply to gather myself and conclude the story for him.

"We admitted him into psychiatric care for three days, then outpatient counseling, and antidepressants that he's still on now."

"I'm so sorry that happened, Marcos. But at least he is over it."

"Yes, but after your child tries to end their life, you are never the same. You are always on guard and your mind automatically goes to the worst places. 'What is he doing in his room? What does his bad mood mean? Am I going to drive home from your apartment one day and find him hanging from our tree swing?' But eventually, you land on a commitment to your child—it may be scary, it may be confusing, but you have to love them and choose to support them 100 percent."

"He's lucky to have a dad like you. Have you seen him process his struggles through his art with you?"

"Yes, I have," I said, brightening a bit as I remembered drawing next to him. "His art is very beautiful but different— even a little scary sometimes. One day I see him drawing a rat in human clothing doing all these cool things. Then the next day he sketches abstract human bodies that unravel like ribbons as if they are trying to undo their creation. They are amazing. He has such a mastery of anatomy, and his renderings are stunning. But when I sit with him, I can sense his pain. It's the pain of being in the wrong body."

"I can't imagine. Marcos, what do you do when you see that from him?" Joe asked, his eyes wetting with emotion.

"Well, I hold his sketchbook and tell him what I like about his art. Then I ask him how he feels about it. One time he told me, 'My body doesn't seem real. I look at it and my head just splinters when I can't make sense of who the hell *that* person in the mirror is. Then I peel myself like sharpened pencil shavings that twist

172

into a bloody mess as I work toward a recognizable core.' I mean, what do you do with that? It's beautiful, but so tortured. I look at the images and I can see how he's suffering inside—his art is a window into his inner world."

"I understand your interest in art therapy now," Joe said, looking over at me. "Pain likes to hide in the shadows and let fear take all the limelight. Most people keep their pain bottled up until it pops out like a boogeyman. Elliott is brave to share that part of himself. Is he okay now?"

How many times a day do I ask myself that same question? "I think so. I talk to him about it more now. When he came out as trans and got bullied, he was spiraling down and I couldn't see it. Now we talk more openly about depression being a spiral. 'Where are you on the spiral? Are you going up or down?' That's how I try to gauge if he is getting darker or getting lighter."

"Light or dark . . . it's a choice," Joe stated.

I bristled at his simplification of what my family was dealing with. "I have dealt with depression for years," I rebutted. "You don't just choose to be happy. That's not how it works."

"I know that, but hear me out," Joe urged. "Don't let your problem *become* the problem."

"What does *that* mean?"

"Problems can become negative when you focus on them with fear. Do you remember when I told you that *fear* loves to be the star—out front, driving all the action? Well, *problems* are fear's favorite costars. Problems can focus all your attention in one place, usually a dark place. And once you're there, your vision starts to narrow until nothing else matters. Then fear jumps in and makes the problem bigger until all your energy revolves around it. You start digging deeper and deeper into the problem and it just gets darker and darker."

"So what should I do, ignore it?"

"No, don't ignore it, just put the problem in its place. You don't have to stay in the dark place you are both in right now," Joe said, tapping his fingers on the black dash. "It's like the 'You Are Here' map at the mall. You've seen them, right?"

"Yes, of course. The one with the red dot."

"Well, life is just like that. When you stand in front of the map, you are on the red dot. But you don't have to stay there. You can move, you can change. Whether you choose to move yourself or your outlook on something like a big problem, you can just pick up your red dot where you are now and move it to the place you want. It's easy to just stop, realize where you are, let go of that place, pull back from it, and then move to a new one. Most people never understand this, and they remain stuck in one spot."

"Well, I can't just imagine that this isn't a problem."

"It *is* a problem, and a dangerous one!" Joe assured. "But it doesn't define you, or Elliott. Do you think your son wants to be known as the kid who was going to kill himself? No! Who is Elliott without the darkness of his depression?"

I pictured Elliott standing in his black clothing and clunky combat boots as I searched for an answer.

"What do you love about him?" Joe asked.

"He has a deep and sensitive heart. The depth of how he sees the world amazes me and his art is way beyond his

174

age—even when it's hard to look at. But that same troubled heart holds such compassion for other people. He knows what it's like to be an outcast and he befriends isolated and struggling kids at school."

"Wow! That's wonderful," Joe said. "Now who are *you* without this problem?"

I sat at the stoplight, pierced by his question as a weird feeling came over me. I wasn't sure I knew how to answer. I looked over and Joe had a satisfied look on his face.

"You know the answer, Marcos. It's right in front of you."

I had identified with my fear and worry so firmly for so long that I was honestly stuck.

Joe reached over and put his hand on my leg. "Elliott has a compassionate, artistic heart and he is as intelligent as he is brave. He also has a dad who loves him and supports him 100 percent. Isn't that you without the problem?"

All I could focus on at that moment was not blubbering. I nodded and tried to keep my eyes on the road as I pulled into the parking lot at Joe's apartment.

Joe took back his right hand and pointed a finger at the dash again. "You and Elliott don't live over there at the problem," he said, pointing to the right for emphasis before moving his finger toward the center. "You live over here, where the love is. The problem isn't moving, it stays over there. You go and visit your problem when you need to, but always come home to where the love and the light are. That's the trick of picking up your spot and moving it."

I looked over at the dashboard where Joe had drawn his imaginary map and I could see the neighborhood of reaction and fear where I had been living, but I could also recognize the one of love and empowerment next to it. And it was right then, pulling the car to a stop in the handicapped spot, that I decided to move. "I like that, Joe. I'm moving."

"Hold your ground when Elliott goes dark," Joe said, making a fist. "Go get him and walk him back to the right spot on the map."

I felt hope for Elliott for the first time in memory. "How do I do that?"

"Love him, go with him into the dark, but lead him back out. He loves you and trusts you. Recognize what he is doing right and point to that. Point to the strength he shows as he shoulders his burden—point to any move back toward love and light. Positive beats negative, Marcos."

How many opportunities to lead Elliott back from darkness had I missed? I vowed to do the next good thing with him and then search for each new chance going forward. *Would I be able to see more opportunities if I could maintain a positive outlook like Joe does?*

"I love that Elliott helps other kids at school," Joe said, turning to face me and keeping the conversation going after we'd parked. "When you help him, know that you equip Elliott to help others. If he helps someone else, maybe that person goes on to help dozens or even hundreds of others. How would that feel?"

"I hadn't thought about it that way, but I guess it is like a chain. It feels pretty amazing to imagine it."

"It's a chain reaction and it's the most rewarding, most impactful thing I have found in this long life—and I want you and Elliott to have that," Joe said, choking up with emotion as he looked up at me. "Marcos, this is why I push you so hard sometimes. I can see where you are, and I know I can help you get to a better place on your map. What you give me, by driving me, walking with me, cleaning up after me, is worth so much more than the ten dollars an hour I can afford to pay you. These lessons are the only thing I can give you that comes close to what you do for me. *You* are the next good thing for me."

I walked in the front door, eager to engage Elliott and try what Joe had shown me. He had just gotten home from school. He was wearing a black sweater covered in sewed-on patches; some looked homemade. Elliott stood in front of the kettle, just staring at it. I was looking for any way inside.

"Hey, did you paint that patch?" I asked, pointing to a green plant with a blue-black berry in the middle.

He looked at the patch I was pointing to. "It's deadly nightshade. The belladonna—very poisonous. Are you driving tonight?"

Recognize anything that he is doing right and point to that, even if it is toxic. "No, I'm working at home tonight. Elliott, the patch looks amazing. Did you paint any of the other ones?"

He showed me one patch after another—a bloody tooth, a woman's face, a cactus with a flower. I made a tea for myself and followed up on the cactus patch until we were in the living room talking about my struggling potted cactuses. Elliott went from plant to plant, giving me advice on new pots and soil changes. It was easier than I thought once I got him going. "It's that easy," Joe's words came back to me. *Why had I been making things so hard?*

CHAPTER 11

I spent the next week counting down the days until the scheduled interview with Coronado College and hoping that Naropa would get back to me with a date. I helped Joe through his normal routine of lunch meetings, laundry, coaching me, and two doctor visits. The second specialist wrote Joe a new script that we needed to fill the same day, so I drove him to his local pharmacy, and we waited in the car until his medicine was ready.

"Will you need to go inside to pick it up or do you think they will give it to me?"

"This pharmacy knows that I have assistants," Joe said with a laugh. "By now, they'd likely give it to anyone who came through the door. I'll be able to wait here while you get it, but they always call me as soon as it's ready."

"Is it anything serious?"

"Apparently my outlook isn't bright enough, so the doctor prescribed me some happy pills."

"Aah," I said, playing along. "Is *that* your secret?"

"Don't write that in your journal," Joe said, wagging a finger at me.

"Got it," I said with a salute. "I *have* been writing down some other things about you."

"Did you post any of them?" Joe countered quickly.

I smiled and tried to imagine what he would say to keep things positive. "I tried, but the problem is the story keeps getting better and better—so it's hard to know when to stop and capture something. If I had posted what I was going to post three weeks ago, it wouldn't be good enough compared to what I'd write now."

"It sounds like at least one of us is improving then," Joe said with a sidelong glance that broke into one of his trademark smiles. "You'll know when the time is right to share."

"Have you always been this happy and positive?" I asked in what felt like a Joe-caliber question.

Joe's smile changed from levity to pride as he turned to face me. "I have been this happy and positive all of my adult life, but it isn't by accident, Marcos."

"Was it a path you chose at the beginning?"

"Yes," Joe answered, but looked ahead through the windshield at the people walking in and out of the pharmacy. "But it's also a choice that I have to make constantly."

"Like even now, you have to keep choosing to be positive?"

"Sure," Joe said as if the answer were obvious. "I could be upset that my medicine isn't ready and that we have to wait in this miserable parking lot—or I could notice what a beautiful day it is and how I get to enjoy some quality time with someone special to me. I choose what I experience. We all choose, every day, all day. Those choices drive our behavior and our behavior in turn defines our destiny."

"Destiny," I repeated as I looked out with him. "That's a heavy word to throw around in a pharmacy parking lot."

"See that woman," Joe said, pointing to a lady who had just dropped her phone while getting into her car.

"Yeah, that's a bummer. She looks frustrated."

"No, look at her body language, her tilted head, her shoulders slumped in resignation. That's well-practiced behavior. She's been like this many times before and she's familiar with this experience. She will probably choose to act the same way several times today. She is creating a frustrating destiny for herself that she is completely unaware of. Frustrated people have frustrating lives."

What the heck? Did he see this everywhere he went? I wondered as I studied the woman's behavior while she picked up her phone in a huff.

"Remember Mr. Fancy Car who almost ran over us?" Joe asked.

"Yeah, *he* was angry, but *we* were the ones who could have been hurt."

"He likely chose that behavior over and over until it defined him. Angry people have angry lives."

"I remember I was really upset," I said, recalling my emotion from the incident. "But you acted differently."

"I made a different choice than you. Our choices eventually catch up with us. Just look at me," Joe said, pointing to himself. "Happy people have happy lives."

I looked over at him as he studied other shoppers leaving the pharmacy. He did seem to be leading a happy life.

Then Joe turned and looked at me. "And sad people have sad lives."

Bam! I knew that was meant for me. His words struck a nerve as I thought about the choices I had been making up to now. Here I was lamenting my unemployment, my brutal interview, my depression, my suicidal son, my empty bank account—while sitting beside me was a bent-over, half-paralyzed, unable to get around octogenarian facing the end of his life, who just kept making the positive choice at every turn. *That* was his secret. I looked over at him and every ounce of self-pity I was carrying just dropped. I wanted a new destiny.

"Aah, that's the call," Joe said, handing me two twenties. "Get some vanilla Ensures and some candy bars for me too, please."

The kids were home on summer break, and I started to watch Elliott more closely as a change in his medication caused him to become more lethargic and moodier than normal. I came home after the errands with Joe to find both Elliott and Lilly staring at their phones, still in their pajamas on the couch exactly where I had left them hours before. They both grunted at me as I walked in, neither bothering to look up from their scrolling. "Man, what a life," I snapped. "You haven't moved from when I left."

"It's summer break, Dad," Lilly protested. "Let me emphasize *break*, as in give me a . . ."

I stood there, determined to get them moving. "Come on, you grubs! This can't be what you are doing with our lives." I pointed to the pug snoring on the floor. "Look at that sad potato. Let's take her for a walk."

The word *walk* was all it took to snap little Zuzu out of her coma. If I couldn't get the kids moving, the pug's glassy, bulging eyes would. Not even Elliott could resist those mournful dog eyes and within minutes both of them were up and ready to go. We loaded Zuzu and drove to our favorite family spot near a small lake circled by mature trees that gave way to a string of newly built upscale mansions. The dog knew the route well and she was barking with excitement as we parked under the first large trees, only to shoot out of the first opened door in a dead run toward the lake. Lilly chased after her with the leash while Elliott and I followed behind.

"This place is so beautiful, it looks like one of those stock images people must use in ad work," Elliott said. "It would be perfect if it weren't for the McMansions popping up everywhere."

"I think some of them have cool designs, but I wouldn't live in something that big—even if I had that kind of money," I said, looking for a way to connect with Elliott to see where his mental state was.

"If I had that kind of mad money, I wouldn't change anything for us," Elliott said. "I would just pay off our house so you could relax and be yourself."

Is that what it would take for me to be myself? I wondered as we walked. "Seriously, Elliott, what would you want to do in life if you were rich?"

"Art," he said, without hesitating. "I would just do what I want to do—and what I want to do is create art. Dad, imagine just waking up and doing art all day."

"I *can* imagine it because I *do* art all day—when I'm working."

Elliott laughed. "You do art for hire—it's different."

Well, at least he's got that figured out, I mused to myself as I watched my daughter run after Zuzu. "Lilly, keep that dog out of the pond," I shouted down to her. "If she gets wet it will stink up the car and I'm rideshare driving tonight."

"She always smells like an old shrimp boat after her swims," Elliott chuckled.

It felt good to hear him laugh. I went back to our topic to try to open him up. "So, you wake up, you have no school and no job at the plant store. You have just time and art supplies—what do you do? Would you create work for galleries? Would you want to illustrate medical books or botany guides?"

He just shook his head. "Those sound like jobs. Remember, I'm rich. So, no offense, but I don't want to pimp my art through others. I'd be content to fill hundreds, eventually thousands of sketchbooks and die an old art hermit—leaving the world an art hoard of bizarre oddities."

184

"You could definitely do that," I said. "I'm not going to lie, that sounds kind of cool."

I loved talking to him, but it wasn't getting to the kind of probing question Joe could always ask to open someone up, so I just asked the one question that had worked best on me. "Why do you think you are here, Elliott?"

He walked beside me and looked down at the path in front of us. "I'm still not convinced that I want to be here."

His honesty stunned me, and I turned away so that he couldn't see the emotion on my face. I felt like I had walked straight into a door. *Were we back here again?* I wondered with dread and then remembered my last lesson from Joe. *Recognize where you are on the map and move that spot to where you want it.* "Go and get

Elliott when he goes dark and bring him back to the home spot where the love and the light are," Joe's words echoed inside me.

"I appreciate you sharing with me where you're at right now," I said, trying to build a bridge to where he was. "Life is hard sometimes, Elliott. I have been going through a rough patch since I lost my job, but we have to keep going. It gets better."

"How are things getting better for you?"

Here's the opening—don't fumble this, I said to myself as I matched his strides. "I've been working on my outlook and my depression, and some things are coming into focus for me. I listened to a story on NPR recently that a scientist had calculated that our odds of being born at this time, in this place, to our parents are something like four hundred trillion to one. So, when I think of that and remember that I have lived over fifty years just so that I could walk beside you in this beautiful spot, I realize that each of us is here for a reason. I think I'm getting a little closer to mine."

Elliott stopped walking and gestured at Lilly, who was watching Zuzu happily chugging along in the water. "Shrimp boat."

He flopped down in the grass beside the trail and moved over for me to sit next to him. "I don't know, Dad. It's different being in the wrong body. Every time I look in the mirror, I wish I was seeing something different."

I thought back to Joe's course question that turned around a doubting room: *What problem are you here to solve?* I had seen Joe use it to turn people's focus from themselves to service for others in a way that pointed them toward their purpose. "I hear the pain in your voice, Elliott. Do you think you can help other people who feel the same way about their bodies?"

He watched Lilly playing with Zuzu in the water. "I would love to help people with their transitions. I love anatomy, but I'm no surgeon."

"Are there other ways to help?" I asked.

"Well, there might be one way. I've been thinking about tattoos more and more recently," Elliott said, perking up a bit as if visualizing some new art.

He loved looking at other people's tattoos and asking about their piercings. "Why tattoos?" I asked.

"Body modification and tattoos are changes too, but it's just changing the outside to match what's on the inside."

"I never thought about it that way. Would you want to put your art on other people? That could be cool. You have the talent for it, Elliott."

"I've thought about it, but I don't want to be stuck tattooing butterflies or phrases like 'not all who wander are lost' over and over on Instagram girls."

"Well, you have to pay your dues in any art form," I said, watching Lilly start walking back up with the dog. "Maybe there's something special you could do."

"Some tattoo artists have been volunteering their work to cover up female to male gender-affirming surgery scars," Elliott volunteered. "But it would work for any other type of scar too."

My mind flashed back to the red scars and numerous bandages that started appearing on him after his first attempt. The outpatient psychologist had called them self-harm scars, inflicted as a physical release from unseen emotional pain. Elliott just called them cutting. *Get him and bring him back to the right spot on the map.* "Wow, that would be amazing. That could really help people who need it. You could totally do that. What would you need to start? Art school?"

"No," Elliott dismissed. "I think you have to find a tattoo artist who you can apprentice under. I heard it's pretty tough. You're like someone's gopher and art monkey for years as you learn enough to do it yourself."

"You could tattoo me once you get the hang of it."

Elliott laughed. "What would you want? A flaming ukulele? A flamenco dancer?"

I soaked in his fresh joy as he teased me. "How about a hula girl, but in that 1940s style, like I'd just gotten out of the navy or something."

Lilly overheard our joking conversation and joined in. "Dad, are you getting a tattoo?"

"Yes, I'm going to be Elliott's first customer."

"Oh, you should get a unicorn," Lilly offered.

"I could do a tramp stamp on you," Elliott joked. "Maybe something inspirational to match this new positive outlook you've had recently."

"I love this idea," Lilly chimed in. "But it should be something classy like 'No Regrets.'"

"But I could intentionally misspell it like Dad always misspells things."

"'No Regerts.'" Lilly chuckled.

"I could so easily do that and you wouldn't know," he said with a mischievous grin.

"I'd be open to a tramp stamp that looks like yellow tape and reads 'Police Line: Do Not Cross.'"

I smiled and enjoyed their riffing laughter as they continued to imagine inappropriate ink on me. Searching for the next good thing had started me down this new path with Joe where he was showing me how to break old patterns in my life and look for what was good, confident, and hopeful instead. And now, I was finding it everywhere—like in the teasing laughter of my children.

Pride filled my heart to hear Elliott recognize a change in me. *I was changing—I could feel it.* It hadn't been a quick conversion, but more of a slow evolution of the soul as I spent more and more time with Joe. And the more I tried to use what Joe was teaching me, the more opportunities I found to do the next good thing. I was noticing so much more beauty and joy in my kids. *Had it been there all along? Were depression and old patterns building blind spots to this goodness?* The more I recognized it in them, the more space it seemed to create for them to grow and thrive. *How much judgment and pressure had I projected on them with fears like "Is Elliott eyeing the knives again?" and "How can I pay for cheerleading?"*

There was always room for laughing, hanging out, and real joy like today—whether I had enough money or not.

I had just dropped off my first rider for the night when I got a message from friends to join them and some others for dinner at an upscale Mexican restaurant in a trendy neighborhood—their treat. Two free meals in one day was something I could get used to. I toggled off my driver availability in the app and drove toward downtown, which would be primed for riders after dinner.

My friends Eric and Desiree were sitting in a large booth with two friends from their neighborhood, Pete and Jill. I met them once at a party at Eric's house and we got reacquainted as the appetizers arrived.

"Order anything you want, Marcos," Desiree said to me. "We just ordered."

Tall and tanned Pete had just received a promotion and Jill was about to start a tutoring business. I volunteered the recent developments in my ongoing job search and that I drive for Uber.

Bookish and nerdy Jill asked the usual question about ride-share driving. "What is the craziest thing anyone has ever done in your car?"

"I guess I'm lucky, but the most bizarre thing was a cowboy serenading his girlfriend. It was cute. Despite all the horror stories out there, I find that people are generally kind."

"Marcos has been providing elder home care for a man who had a stroke. He's been doing it for several months now," Eric interjected. "How long has it been?"

"Like four or five months," I answered between bites.

"Tell them about it," Desiree prompted.

I looked around the black and white Mexican murals on the red walls as I thought about how to begin the crazy story for them. "It started as a mix of altruism and desperation. Funds were getting really tight, and I had been out of work for several months already. I found a posting on social media that said 'Help Our

Friend Joe,' so I replied. The pay is terrible. I haven't made that kind of money since the eighties, but it just felt right somehow."

"I'm all for helping out," Eric said. "But you have to keep the lights on, my friend. It's time to get back to that career."

I knew he was right but staying in my routine with Joe seemed right in a different way. "I'm working on it. I have an interview in a few days and another one pending. Fingers crossed," I added.

"That's great news," Eric said, raising a glass. "Here's to getting back on track."

Clinking my glass with everyone, I couldn't help but feel that "back on track" for me was more to do with Joe's lessons than any job offer. "Well, I didn't really know what I was doing. I took the caregiving job through a leap of faith of sorts, but so far, it's been a life-changing experience for me."

"Life-changing," Jill said. "In what ways?"

"Well, I went into this thinking that I am helping a guy get through his life after this crippling injury and he ends up helping me get through my own crippling life issues like depression and fear."

"Really?" Pete asked. "How does he do that?"

"Well, I'm still trying to piece that all together, but I live with the results of it every day," I said, not exactly sure how to describe it. "Joe is just amazing. He can't take care of his daily needs and he faces a lot of struggles, but then everywhere he goes he is just the center of attention. He just has this ability to pull everyone into his dynamo of positive energy. It's like a magic trick, but with people."

THE NEXT GOOD THING

"Didn't you say he was a motivational speaker?" Desiree asked.

"Yes, and I think in some ways he still is. He's motivating the heck out of me—and it's working."

"Positive thinking is great," Pete countered. "But you have to be realistic. Jill, what was that article you read to me last week? 'Fake It Until You Make It' or something like that? It was about how pretending things are better was actually detrimental to a person's progress."

"The article was called 'Fake It Until You Mistake It,'" Jill corrected.

I could feel their doubt about Joe's impact on me and others—but I was the only person at the table who emptied pee bottles for a living. I tried to channel Joe at that moment as I searched for a way to communicate all that was happening to me. *Doubtful people have doubtful lives.* "I agree with you. But I think Joe is realistic in how he helps people address their problems and challenges through making good decisions that foster positive attitudes and outcomes. The problem is always there, front and center, and you have to deal with it, but he reframes the situation in a way that something helpful can come from it. It takes all the negative energy away from the problem and redirects it toward some positive outcome. It's like a judo move."

I could see the questions in their eyes above their salted margarita rims.

"Many of us experience pain or trauma because of some current or past problem," I continued. "Joe looks at that pain as a clue that points to the problem, but then he starts that person thinking about how they might be able to help others who are experiencing that same pain they are. And if they can do that, what meaning or purpose might that bring to their lives? How might their life be impactful or rich by discovering that and then pursuing it?"

"A follow your dreams kind of thing?" Pete asked.

"Joe believes everyone is here for a reason and not finding our life's work is a life only half lived."

"I don't know about that," Pete challenged. "I really wanted to be a teacher. Adult literacy was a problem that I was passionate about. I got my teaching certificate and taught for five years."

"And what happened?" I asked, feeling Joe's contagious enthusiasm in my question.

"Those were great years, but I was broke," Pete said. "I tried to solve one problem and it created another. So I got this data analysis job and now I make three times my teacher's salary—problem solved."

"Yeah, but the pressure is driving you crazy," Jill said.

"I get the whole money thing, I do. I will drive drunks home after dinner for less than the tip will be. But is your data job just a different problem now—perhaps one that pays but that doesn't reward?"

I could tell from his reaction that Pete still had some pain about walking away from his educator dream. "My normal career, as Eric mentioned earlier, is in graphic design—or art for hire as my kid describes it. Part of that career was in advertising, so I get the crazy stress thing. My first creative director had a heart attack before fifty. I enjoyed parts of the work, and it paid well, but I feel like it cost me some parts of my soul."

Pete looked at me like he understood my point. "I wouldn't say I have to sell my soul, but I do check it at the door of DataVis every morning. I guess it's just easier to leave it at home after a while."

"Maybe DataVis needs a 'Bring Your Soul to Work Day,'" Desiree said with a sly smile.

Jill chimed in after we finished laughing. "It's kind of sad that office environments are so tough on people. Even my nonprofit has brutal office politics."

We went on for most of the dinner on how hard most of their jobs were. I tried to think of what Joe would say and interjected a few times. "I think it circles back to the judo flip to the positive, even if the situation is stressful or overwhelming. It's like an air supply for your soul," I said. "That kind of positivity can fill a room; I've seen Joe do it. It allows everyone there to be their best."

"What do you think Joe would say if he were here crushing tacos with us right now?" Pete asked.

"Joe would say, being the most positive person in the room is a gift to everyone on your team," I said, satisfied that Joe would approve.

"Wow, I love that challenge," Jill said, her face lighting up. "Be the most positive person in the room. I like that."

193

Pete laughed. "I like the way that sounds too, but what if my boss expects me to just walk in and start kicking ass?" he said sarcastically.

"Oh, you kick ass," Eric joked. "You *positively* kick ass."

Leaving the restaurant, I toggled on my ridesharing app and snapped up a rider request from a nearby bar to a distant suburb— nearly a hundred-dollar ride. It was two soccer mom types in their forties who had just closed down a bar.

"Okay, Uber Marcos, please take us home," Sue said as they got into my car. "I need you to drop off Cindy on the way. But don't worry, we're good tippers."

"That's fine. It happens all the time. Just tell me where to go."

"We never go out like we used to," Cindy confessed. "We both have young kids now, so when we do it gets a little crazy."

I could tell they were both a bit drunk. They laughed like teenagers, proud of their night's adventures. Sue was the first to comment on the music I was playing. "What are we listening to? Is that a jazz harp?"

The tone of her question let me know she was not a fan. "It's Alice Coltrane, John's wife. I can change it if you want."

"Do you like jazz?" Cindy chimed in.

"Yes."

"Do you like Charlie Mingus?"

"I don't know him."

Cindy leaned forward in the seat and looked at me. "Good God, man!"

I grabbed my phone and used a voice command to play Mingus. After a short chime, the car filled with soulful jazz.

Cindy smiled and sank back into the seat as the music picked up. "Right? So good. He played with everybody, Miles, Dizzy, Monk, Horace Parlan."

"Who?"

"Okay, Parlan's next."

Sue leaned forward and whispered in my ear as Cindy closed her eyes and took in the music. "Maybe you should drop me off first."

I played jazz as we drove south and occasionally answered a question from the back seat when they wanted an affirming opinion on something. I followed the map to Sue's house and dropped her off.

Cindy told me which way to go as I put on her next selection. "Are you married?"

I turned down the music a bit. "No, I'm divorced."

"I'm not happy," she blurted out. "My husband is a great dad, but I don't know if I have ever been happy."

I could feel the pain in her words as we drove. "I know about not being happy. I know about depression. It's like a hole in a balloon that lets all your life leak out."

She smiled, but I had the feeling she wished I would just keep driving.

"I heard something today that really snapped my head around about how I was creating a life I didn't want."

"Lay it on me."

"An old man who is very special said to me, 'sad people lead sad lives.'"

"Well, that's me," Cindy said. "But he missed the part about how tough circumstances make people sad."

"That's the thing, Cindy. He didn't leave that out. That was his point." I described Joe and how I cared for him daily.

"So what's this old man's secret?"

Well, I know it isn't pills, I chuckled to myself. "He chooses happiness. Every morning he sets his mind on the encouragement and optimism he can share with others, and then throughout the day he makes positive and loving choices in how he reacts to things and how he interacts with people."

"Is that hard to do?"

"*He* makes it look easy. I mean, here I am helping him walk where he goes, cleaning up after him, but this stooped and broken old man is like a movie star wherever he goes as everyone reacts to the love and positivity he radiates. When I compared myself to him, I felt like a self-indulgent little punk for feeling sorry for myself. I've been thinking about this all day."

"And what did you come up with?" Cindy asked.

I listened to Joe's stinging words again in my head. *Was this my next choice? What was the next good thing here?* "Yes, I'm sick of my sad sack life. That isn't why I'm here. So, I am deciding, right now," I affirmed, "to start making different choices in how I relate to people and how I handle new challenges when they come up. The way we act every day eventually becomes how we live—I think that's what he meant. I choose to be happy."

"I could use some of that," she sighed.

I looked at her in the mirror as we approached her house. "Marriage is tough, especially with kids. It's easy to give all your energy to your kids because you just love the stuffing out of them. My wife and I did that. I relied on the structure of marriage to keep us going and I didn't cultivate our relationship. Before I knew it, it had crumbled. I think if I had showed up every morning being happy and loving, things could have been different."

Cindy sat in the back seat and looked out the window at her house and I imagined that she was inventorying a selection of possible choices. "Thanks. I needed that," she said, opening the door. "Best Uber ride ever—five stars."

I just laughed. "You're going to be great."

CHAPTER 12

I buzzed with excitement as I drove toward the campus of Coronado Christian University. I had delivered Uber Eats there a few times, so I knew just where to go. My thoughts bounced between seeing a paycheck deposited into my bank account and wondering what creative work would be like in a Christian context. I had spent lots of years in the church; my parents even hosted a youth group once a week for years while I was in high school. I knew all the Christian lingo favorites like "praying a hedge of protection," "believers," "humbled," and "quiet time" and readied my Christianese vocabulary. I was ready to nail this.

Walking into the white marbled lobby, a graduate student greeted me and then walked me back to the meeting room. She stayed with me for a few minutes until the interviewers came in. I felt nervous but sharing a coffee and talking about her spiritual journey at Coronado really put me at ease. She was amazing and her description of their culture of making spiritual health a priority, where love and grace are lived out daily as part of "the Christian walk," reminded me of the good parts of Christianity that I missed. My heart felt so hopeful, and I looked forward to being a part of it again. *Would this be like coming home?* I wondered.

David, the creative director I had spoken to on the phone, came in looking surprisingly cool in a print T-shirt and Carhartt jeans. He looked like a hip youth pastor and all I could think of was: *It's time to ditch the slacks and sport coat for good.*

"Marcos, welcome," David said, offering a firm handshake. "Our writer and designer will be right here. We reviewed your work, and we really like your portfolio."

"That's nice to hear," I said, relieved.

"Marcos, this is Beth," David said, introducing us.

Beth was blond and looked a few years older than David and wore an ankle-length red and white print dress. "It's so nice to see you," Beth said. "I do the design work and I am also a copywriter."

"Wow, both," I said. "That's a strong combination, but one I don't see very often. I can write copy too but be warned—I can't spell my way out of a wet paper bag."

"Neither can he," she said with a smile at David, who I guessed was her boss.

David started the interview. "Marcos, your print experience has pushed you to the top of our candidate list. We need someone who is comfortable with that side of things. Can you talk about that a bit more?"

"Sure. I've done a lot of prepress work, including press checks and making sure everything is bombproof. It pays to get that stuff straight before the presses start cranking out copies."

"Great," Beth chimed in. "If you pre-check my files, I will proofread your spelling."

They are already talking about working with me, I thought as they asked other questions about my background and how I had solved design and production problems in the past. I felt a huge weight lift from me as they opened the topic of compensation and made an offer of 30 percent more money than I had been making at my last job.

David seemed ready to close the deal on me. "Marcos, you seem like a good fit for the role, but I want to talk about the creative culture here at Coronado. I was on the agency side for years and I want you to know that the culture here is very different from what you might have been used to in your last shop."

That was a relief. I really liked them both and could see myself working well with them. A warm and welcoming excitement rose inside me.

"We're a faith-based college," David continued. "I'm sure you read our mission statement."

I nodded.

"How does that align with your life and mission?"

"I agree with your mission of advancing God's purpose in this world."

"That's great. I'm glad to hear that, but how does that align with what's going on with you?" David said, raising his hand to touch his heart. "In here."

How much should I share about where I am right now? Do they expect me to be a Christian to work here? Would they be saving me a place next to them on the pew on Sunday morning? "My mission right now is to look for the next good thing and then do that. Like right now, I am providing home care for an older gentleman. I guess you can say I found him through a leap of faith when I asked for guidance." I covered my heart with my right hand.

"I asked to be here, at this table with you—and that request was answered. I believe in God, but I don't think of myself as a Christian anymore. I haven't considered myself one in seven years. I still value God and I seek Him, but it doesn't look like my former Christian walk."

Beth leaned forward and put her arms on the table. "Do you believe in God or are you struggling with your faith?"

That was a good question and one that I didn't ask myself very often. "I do believe in God. When I was walking the Christian walk, I struggled with my faith a lot. But now I just let God be God and I try to be the best person I can be. It's way easier now and in some ways my relationship with Him has never been better."

"Can you tell me more about that?" David asked.

"I spent the majority of my adult life as a Christian who was trying to be more like Christ. It's hard, and I wasn't very good at it. In the end, I realized Christ is better at being more like Christ—and I am more comfortable just being a good Marcos. My prayers keep getting answered, so God must like having a good Marcos around."

David chuckled, but I felt like it was to ease some silent tension building on his side of the table from not getting the exact answers he wanted. "Being more like Christ is super challenging. It sounds like you are still on your path. Being here at Coronado might be perfect for you."

"Yes, it might. I feel very comfortable here and I look forward to working with you both."

"There are some final things I need to ask you. Our culture here at Coronado is very important to us. Like I said earlier, we think you're a great fit for the job and are ready to move forward today; we just need to make sure you're a good fit for Coronado."

"Sure," I answered, hoping I could stay inside their lines as they drew them.

"We have a dress code at the college, for students and staff. Are you okay adhering to a policy of modest and respectable apparel at all times?"

I looked down at my sport coat and pants as I thought about how to answer. *Was I that out of touch?*

"Oh, you're fine, Marcos," Beth interrupted. "It's more about female students in short skirts and boys in cutoff T-shirts."

"Yes, I'm fine with that. I mean, no cutoffs or miniskirts for me," I joked.

David continued, "The next questions are about living a biblical lifestyle, specifically no drinking or drugs. The passage we use for guidance is Ephesians 5:18: 'Do not get drunk on wine, for that is debauchery. Instead, be filled with the Spirit.' Is that okay?"

Is it okay if that spirit is a single malt scotch? I asked internally. "I don't have a problem with drinking, but I do like to have a beer after mowing the lawn. Is that going to be a problem?"

Beth jumped in again. "No, this is more about drunkenness and marijuana now that it's legal here in Colorado."

"Sure, I'm okay with that. No to getting drunk, yes to being with God," I said, feeling a bit of discomfort and hoping this question would be the end of it.

"All right, this next one is a little more personal," David pressed. "Do you uphold a biblical guide for sexual relations, meaning only within the sanctity of marriage?"

I thought about the question and feared the ones that might follow it.

"Basically, this means not living with someone," David offered in a tone that aimed to downplay the intrusion of the question. "I know these are personal questions. We ask them to make sure you are committed to your walk with God."

Would I ever live with a woman, or would I ever be married again? I wondered. I didn't like where these questions were going, but a good-paying job hung in the balance. "Ask for it," Joe's words came back to me. *I had asked to sit in this seat across from them. Was being here now an answered prayer?* The chances of me living with a woman in the next year seemed astronomical. *Just get the damned job.* "I don't think we have to worry about that one."

"I think I know the answer to the next one," David joked. "Do you embrace a homosexual lifestyle?"

203

My heart sank as he finished the question. *Why did they care about this? Did they really think that Jesus would love a gay or lesbian person any less than a leper or a prostitute?* I felt sad as I imagined all of those who they would lock out of God's house. I thought about how badly I wanted this job as I fidgeted in the chair. *Technically, I wouldn't be lying if I answered just for myself.* "No," I chuckled, trying to match his joking tone. "But I do love a good musical."

David smiled and I hoped that was his last question. *Could these guys even be aware enough of trans issues to have those conduct questions on their biblical watch list?*

"One final question," David began, the smile now gone from his face. "Do you identify with your biological sex?"

. . . and we're falling. I felt the floor give way underneath me as his words hit me. *Why did they have to go there?* I couldn't let this stand. *Was this God's intended reply to my ask?* I let out a sigh that I hoped would strengthen me enough to do the next good thing for my family. "Luckily, I do identify with my biological sex, but I think the term you are looking for is gender. David, Beth, I also identify as the loving father to a transgender son. My son is not as lucky as I am. He wakes up every day struggling with life in the wrong body."

I looked up as David leaned back in his seat. Beth's mouth hung open. "I wish you could know what the smallest kindness means to his daily struggle. A simple smile, a friendly greeting, an open mind, a heart filled with God's love. But you can't know that, because of your"—I stammered as I struggled to finish the sentence. "You want to have the love of God here, but on whose terms?" I asked, leaving the question to hang in the air around us. "You're hiding. But you're also hiding his love behind that code of yours."

"Marcos, I'm really sorry about this," Beth apologized.

"I could never work at a place where my family wouldn't be welcomed," I said, rising on unsteady legs. "I wish you could see how intolerant you seem right now. I'll see myself out."

As I drove home, I replayed my reaction over and over. *Did I do the right thing? Could I have handled things in a way that could have skirted the truth and won me the job?* I felt defeated that the job was right in front of me only to see it fall away. I felt disappointed that my career was still stuck in neutral. But most of all,

I was disappointed in them. *How beautiful would it have been to show God's love to outsiders?*

I walked through my front door and Lilly was on the couch talking on her phone. I needed a boost and had hoped I could talk to one of my kids.

"Hey, Dad, Jess is coming over for lunch. Can we give her a ride back after you get back from Joe's?"

I nodded and sat in the chair across from her.

Lilly smiled and went back to her conversation on the phone. "My dad can drop you back home. I'll see you in a bit."

She set the phone down and looked over at me—a failure in out-of-date pants. "Did you get the job?"

"Nope!"

Lilly winced. "Did they see that 'Fritter Critter' donut ad from back in the day? Total cringe, Dad."

"No," I chuckled, remembering that she hated that one. "Everything was great. I basically had the job until they brought out their code of conduct questions."

"And you failed that?" Lilly asked.

"It's a Bible college, so it's their way of making sure people are Charlie Church enough for them. 'Don't drink, don't live with a woman you're not married to, and don't live a homosexual life-style.' That sort of stuff."

Lilly sat up on the couch and laughed. "Well, number one, don't drink on the job. Number two, women aren't exactly beating down your door, so you're safe there. And three, maybe just butch it up around the office and you'd be fine."

That was the laugh I was hoping for.

"Dad, it's none of their business."

"Yes, but I couldn't lie to them—especially when they asked the 'T' question."

"They asked about Elliott?" Lilly said with a confused look on her face.

"No, not directly, but they got into the whole sex and gender thing, and I couldn't hide who we are as a family," I said, still wondering if I had done the right thing. "I had hoped for a 'don't ask, don't tell' sort of opportunity, but it didn't go down that way."

"That's messed up," Lilly said. "Christianity is supposed to be about love."

"It is, Lilly. But not everyone is willing to do the hard stuff like forgiveness, acceptance, loving your enemies, and turning the other cheek. Loving on gay people should be the easy part."

She sat back and peeked down at her text updates. "Yes, let people be all sparkles and rainbows. They're the best."

I could tell that Lilly wanted to get back to her friends on the phone and I wanted to throw these pants out before heading over to Joe's.

"Dad," Lilly said, looking up at me as I stood. "Seriously, I'm proud of what you did. And I know others will be too."

I knocked on Joe's door and said hello as I let myself in.

"Aah, Marcos, come in here. I want to hear all about it," Joe said from the living room. "How did the interview go, did you nail it?"

"I did nail it," I said, feeling like I *had* interviewed well. "But I didn't get the job."

"No? What happened?"

"They have a code of conduct that wouldn't be accepting of my family," I said, raising my hand to wave. "So, I guess it's bye-bye, Coronado. They could say hello to Bramble Fire on their way out."

"Did you end the interview or did they?" Joe asked.

"I did," I affirmed, still fuming from what felt like both a judgment and rejection.

"Good for you, Marcos," Joe said, motioning me to sit down. "Do you want to talk about it?"

I did. I described how the interview started with them using positive language about working with me, to my print back-ground, and then things going off the rails when their code got exclusionary and hateful. I slowly filled with righteous anger as I relayed the events for him. "How could a college call themselves Christian and then just exclude people that make *them* uncomfort-able? Didn't Jesus welcome the undesirables unto him? He even took in a tax collector, for heaven's sake."

Joe listened to my tirade but didn't say a word. "It just felt so judgmental, like they couldn't associate with anyone not like them. Joe, you're a Christian, what do you think?"

Joe leaned forward and held out his hand. "Would you mind, Marcos?"

I got up and went over to take his hand in our well-rehearsed choreography of getting him on his feet. I placed my hand in his, but he didn't pull against me or try to stand up—he just sat and held my hand. "What are you doing?" I asked, confused.

"When you were sitting over there, you were angry and full of judgment at what happened to you this morning. Then you asked me what I thought. That was an invitation to join you over there, but I didn't go. Instead, I invited you to join me over here, where we aren't angry or judging," Joe said with a smile as he swung our hands back and forth. "It's better over here, isn't it?"

Joe's motion with my hand felt like an invitation to play, but his smile silently communicated *checkmate*. "The spot on the map lesson," I conceded.

He nodded and then waited for a second before speaking. "I know what I do can look easy, but it takes work to remain positive. I maintain it by staying on my spot on the map. I can come to where you are for a visit to try to lead you back to where I am, but I can't stay where you are. If I did, I couldn't be me and more importantly I wouldn't be able to help anyone. Staying on a good spot is the trick."

I stood there holding another man's hand as it hit me. *Joe's consistent positivity isn't magic—he works at it, he wills it. Where would I be now if he didn't work at positive beating negative?*

"So it only looks like 'it's that easy' then?" I joked.

He chuckled and gave a short nod. "Marcos, do you want to hear one of the most powerful words in the English language?"

I returned his smile. I *was* feeling better over where Joe was. "Sure, Joe."

He looked up at me and said, "*Next.*"

"Next?" I asked.

"Yes. *Next* means there's something more, *next* means there's another chance, *next* means there's another person, and *next* means there's another time. It's the most empowering word in the language," Joe said, pulling his hand back. "You try it."

What would be my next opportunity? What would be my next chance? What would be the next good thing? I chuckled as I fell back into my chair. "Next."

"I bet that felt good. Better say it again, Marcos."

"Next!" I said, louder this time.

"I think you've got it. I bet you're thinking about dozens of possibilities that are next for you," Joe said, looking up at the ceiling. "What is the next interview, the next job, the next artwork?"

I looked at him and nodded.

"Well, *I* know what's next for you," Joe said in a serious tone that got my full attention. "Next is taking care of those pee bottles—they aren't going to empty themselves."

I laughed out loud and felt the entire morning fall behind me. "Next," I said, gripping the first bottle within reach.

"I got ya," Joe said with a grin. "Come over and get me up and I'll buy you a big lunch today."

Elliott wanted to hang out with some friends so I agreed to drop him off after I took Lilly's friend home, but I really hoped that I could get that time to talk and check in on him. I turned to him after Lilly closed the door. "Where to?"

"There's a café downtown called Insurrection."

"I know it. I've been there a few times. Who are you meeting?"

"I'm meeting Gabby, she's the only one from the group who's hanging out with me right now, but I also invited this new guy from school to meet us. His name's Clay. He seems pretty cool. And before you ask," Elliott said, turning to look at me, "it is *not* a date, but it could lead to one."

I smiled back at him, but my thoughts kept going back to his group of friends. "Why is Gabby the only one you are hanging out with now?"

"All the others have been hating on me for a while now."

For a while now, I replayed in my head. *Don't miss this. Find out where he is and go bring him back.* "Hating on you? What's that about?"

"A few weeks ago, we were all hanging out at Stephanie's house when they got quiet and then they confronted me together. It was like one of those bad intervention shows. Each of them thought I was making too much out of my mental illness and that I was 'oversharing' with them," Elliott confessed. "Why the hell would I do that? I talk about it with them because it scares the hell out of me. I wake up and it's on me and it stays with me until I fall asleep. So yeah, I guess I talk about it a lot."

"That's what friends are for."

"I know. And it's not like they don't have their problems. Trust me, all those freaks and outcasts have issues too. I listen and I'm happy to give them my time, but when *I* need help, they say I just want attention. Of course I want attention, I want them to listen to me."

"Did you talk to them about it after that?"

"I talked with Gabby on the phone a few times. She's the nicest one. But I decided to wait to talk to Howie and the others until we get my new meds right and I feel a bit more like myself. I can talk to her, but I feel like Howie wants to boot me out. That's why I'm just meeting with her for now. There she is," he said, pointing as he grabbed his sketchbook. "Can you pick me up after driving tonight?"

"Wait a minute, Elliott," I said, reaching out to touch his arm. "I'm worried about you. Should I be?"

Elliott froze for a few seconds as though weighing my words or his reply to them. "I worry about me too sometimes," he volunteered. "Let's draw together later, okay?"

"Sure," I answered as I let go. "I'll call you in a bit to check in on you. Don't have too much coffee."

"Dad, we're teenagers. Caffeine is the only thing that's legal for us."

Downtown Denver was a great starting point for picking up riders. I shuffled people from bar to bar for most of the evening. Everyone was so happy and chatty, and I loved all the short interactions with strangers where I tried to create a Joe-like atmosphere for every rider.

I drove into a nearby neighborhood for a pickup in front of a beautiful art deco apartment building. A man and woman climbed into the back seat. They were laughing as they got in, their pregame festivities clearly underway, and I was about to take off when they stopped me. "No, wait, we have one more. Ernesto, get your butt over here."

A young, good-looking Latino man got in the front seat, and we were off toward a downtown bar. The late-twenties couple in the back were very chatty and kept peppering me with questions about what it was like to drive strangers around. I was about to drop them off when my phone rang, and they could see Elliott come up on the screen in the hands-free holder.

"That's my son," I said in a voice loud enough to get control over the conversation. "He's at a coffee shop nearby with his new friend. I need to take this and check on him if that's okay with you."

"Ooh, is he on a date? Pick him up and let's find out," urged the tipsy woman in the back.

Answering the call, I explained that I had some passengers in the car, and they all yelled out, "Hello, Elliott!"

He asked if I was still downtown and if I could pick him up and take him home. I played along with the passengers' curiosity. "How are things going with Clay?"

Elliott sounded embarrassed and a little upset. "Dad, I will talk to you later. Just come and get me."

"That sounds like a date to me," I said, after hanging up.

The couple in the back got out and started walking toward a bar entrance, but Ernesto stayed behind and looked over at me. "Clay? Is your son gay?"

"He's trans," I answered.

"How old is he?"

"He's in high school."

"So you're okay with your son dating a boy."

"Sure. He can date whoever he wants. I just want him to be happy."

"I'm gay," he blurted out, keeping his dark eyes locked on mine. "My dad stopped speaking to me when I came out. He's that typical macho Latino dad. I think he views his sons as an extension of himself as a man."

"I'm sorry to hear that. How long has it been?"

"Five years. The last time was the day I came out. I sorta knew how he would react, but it still hurt."

"What did he say?" I asked, eager to talk to Ernesto about this if he wanted.

"He didn't say anything at first. Like he couldn't believe it. Finally, he just exploded and said 'Is this who you are? Some faggot? This is not who you are, Ernesto. I have known you since you were born!' It was tough to hear."

"I bet it was. The language we use has power, and sometimes that power can injure." I could see from the emotion on his face that Ernesto had been carrying this for years.

"I put it right back in his face," he added. "'That's right,' I told him to his face. 'I'm a faggot. Your son's a homo.' That's when he lost it. 'Not my son! Not in my house! Get out of my house!' he said before slamming the door on me. And that was it."

"Man, I don't understand how a father could do that. Nothing could stop me from loving my son."

"He *did* love me. That was the thing that hurt," he said, tearing up. "We were close. He came to all my baseball games. We had the same sense of humor. It was good until I told him the truth about me. I don't understand how it can all end with the slam of a door."

I tried to imagine what Joe would say to this beautiful man who was hurting. "Your dad loves you, trust me on that. But he's missing it all. He's missing having a beer with you, seeing you at Christmas, and giving you advice. He's missing out on this," I said, motioning to the two of us sitting in a car. "He's missing just being by your side and talking to you as you go through life. He's making a terrible mistake and he's going to regret it."

Ernesto nodded and looked toward the door of the bar as his friends called out to him. "It just sucks."

Do the next good thing, I heard my inner voice say as he swung open the car door. "In anger, your father used a hateful word to define you. But that is not who you are. Ernesto, you are a man who stood up for himself and risked everything for what is true for you. That took courage. If you were my son, I'd be very proud of how you turned out."

Elliott was standing outside the gritty-looking café when I arrived. He wiped at his cheeks and his eyes looked red like he had been crying. He jumped in the car and just motioned for me to start driving. I started toward home and waited a while before speaking. "Did things not go as planned with Clay?"

"He didn't show."

"I'm sorry about that."

"No, that's the good news," Elliott said with a heavy sigh.

"Was it Gabby then?"

"No, Gabby and I talked and drew together for a while. I was so excited to hang out with her and it was great, but then Howie came in and everything changed. He's always hovering around her. I continued talking to Gabby, while he just radiated anger at me. I brushed it off, but then the rest of the group came in. They said hi and sat down, but then they started talking to Gabby and just ignored me," he relayed as he wiped at his eyes. "I should have just left right then, but I wanted to keep talking to my friend. Couldn't they just let me have one friend?"

"Maybe you can try with just her again?"

"No," Elliott blurted out. "It's over. I blew it."

"What do you mean, you blew it?"

Elliott looked up at the streetlights as we drove south. "I didn't want to show *any* emotion with them, but I was so angry. They didn't have to treat me that way. I got up from the table and looked at some books before getting another tea. When I came back, I could just feel that I wasn't in the group anymore. My heart just broke, right there at the table. That's when I called you."

"I'm glad you did, Elliott."

"But there's more," he offered. "I drank my tea as fast as I could while I gathered up my pencils and sketchbook. I told them I was leaving, and I think they could tell I was inches away from crying. But instead of just letting me go, Howie looked over at me and shook his head. 'Jesus, Elliott, this is a bit dramatic. Why do you always have to be like this? You obviously need a better therapist or something.' Everyone else in the group laughed and that's when I lost it. I don't know what happened, but I just snapped and threw my empty teacup at Howie's head."

"You what?" I asked. "You didn't hit him, did you?"

"It broke on the brick wall over his head, but the pieces landed on him. Everyone just sat there in shock, even Gabby. It was horrible. I just ran out. It's over. I really screwed up this time."

"It will be okay," I said, trying to figure out how it would and what I could say to make my kid feel better right then. *Use the Next lesson? The Map Spot lesson? What positive could beat this negative?*

"Dad, this isn't me," he said in tears. "I don't throw things at my friends' heads."

"Elliott, we're taking you back to the doctor this week to change your medication. Don't worry about those guys right now. Let's focus on getting you back to a good place."

He was quiet until we pulled into the driveway, and I turned off the car. "Don't give up on me," Elliott murmured.

"Never."

CHAPTER 13

The night before my Naropa interview, I researched everything I could about them. I knew their style, their brand, and
their ads. It's so hard to advertise something you don't believe in,
but the more I researched the more I kept saying yes to: contemplative education, introspection, diversity, compassion, creativity,
community. I wanted to be a part of what they were doing.

The next morning, I put on my favorite vintage sport coat, my
favorite blue bow tie, and my favorite comfy pants. I straightened
my tie in the mirror, and I was surprised by the man looking back
at me—I recognized him for the first time in a while. *There he is*,
I thought, admiring the mod '60s jacket. *This guy's ready to get a
dream job today.*

On the drive up to Boulder, I kept thinking about how I would
answer questions about exiting my last job and why I had been
unemployed for so long. My mind kept building airtight alibis
that made me feel less vulnerable, but by the time I reached their
campus I had reviewed every worst-case scenario and was feeling
anxious. I walked around the university grounds in search of a
cup of tea, but the campus café was closed. A few students walked
between the redbrick buildings, moving into and out of sunlight
and shadow. It was quiet and peaceful. I was twenty minutes early,

so I found a beautiful place to sit under two massive sycamore trees in the main square where I took out my journal and began to sketch details of the branches above me. Their limbs stretched out wide, sheltering me from the sunlight. I looked over to the jagged Flatirons mountain peaks that rose vertically at the edge of town, and I took a deep breath before saying aloud, "I want this. Please let me fit in here and get this job." My heart relaxed at that moment as everything around me seemed to say yes.

I entered the redbrick admissions building five minutes early. The young woman behind the reception desk looked up and greeted me with a warm smile. She had tangled dreadlocks and a silver bar through a pierced septum. "Hi, I'm Sheila. Are you here for the tour?"

I couldn't take my eyes off her beautiful hand tattoos. "No, I'm here for the job—the graphic designer job. I'm here to meet with Kelly."

She laughed. "Oh yes, let me get her. Do you want something to drink? I just put on some water for tea."

Even the elusive tea was saying yes. "A cup of tea would be amazing."

Sheila walked back with a woman my age who smiled with her entire face. She came over and shook my hand. "Marcos, I'm Kelly. It's so nice to finally meet you. I love that bow tie. Come with me to the conference room. I will get everyone."

I sat at the long wooden table and studied a giant calligraphy painting on the wall. Sheila came in with a tea for me. "Our founder, Chögyam Trungpa, did that. It's beautiful."

I nodded. "I read that he walked from Tibet to India after the Chinese invasion."

"Yes, he led a group of other monks over the Himalayas in order to save the knowledge from their monastery," Sheila said with pride, before turning toward the door. "It sounds like they are coming. Good luck with your interview."

Kelly walked back into the conference room with four people trailing behind her. There was an ease and warmth in the way they spoke to one another, and it felt to me like they were friends outside of work. She introduced them in turn: David, the multimedia specialist, was first. He was well put together in wools and corduroy and had a boyish kindness about him. Sam and Jon from the web team were next. They wore T-shirts and flannel and bordered on finishing each other's sentences during their introductions. Tall and elegant Cassie, the writer and assistant marketing director, swept into the room last, holding a large coffee. None of them had any paperwork or a copy of my resume or portfolio in front of them. *Was that a good sign?* I wondered as I placed my brown journal in front of me.

"Marcos, this is our creative team," Kelly said. "Can you tell us a little bit about yourself before we start the interview?"

I smiled and took a deep breath. "Well, I'm an artist, a ballroom dancer, a father, and I play a mean ukulele."

"Ukulele, that's cool," David interjected before easing self-consciously back in his seat.

"I think it's cool too," I said, "but my kids think it's too quirky."

"Tell us about what art means to you," Kelly prompted.

"I've always thought art is about capturing the essence of something and preserving it so that others can enjoy it. Art is about seeing through to what's on the inside and making it visible to others. But this past year, I've realized that people can be a form of art when they are able to identify, nurture, and share an inner beauty that attracts everyone around them."

The narrow conference room fell silent, as though each of them were considering my answer.

"I've seen that too," Kelly said. "Thank you for that. I think we should start with the interview questions. I'll start. Marcos, how do you balance multiple projects and deadlines?"

"I typically have at least five projects going at any given time. I set milestones and align project expectations as I go. Most of the time, I can keep from working late if I follow those."

220

"What is something that you could do to help our department right away?" Kelly asked.

"I thought about that," I said. "I reviewed as much of your current content as I could find. I love almost all of it, but I noticed that I didn't see a uniform brand. Brand consistency is important in getting your message out there. The first thing I would do is create a branding strategy with a brand book that we could use internally and share as a guide with vendors and any freelancers we work with."

"How would you contribute to social media work?" David asked.

"Many people think that creative and brand should feed into social media outreach to new and existing consumers, but I have found that Instagram and Twitter can be powerful inputs to the creative. They can be like live testing platforms to see what works and resonates. I love getting that feedback as early as possible."

We discussed proofing, editing, production, and marketing before Cassie asked the first question related to their culture. "Do you think diversity and inclusion are important at a university?"

I flashed back to the last interview for my answer. "Schools that focus on only one type of student unknowingly build blind spots to others who *could* be in their community. How can you serve the whole world when you only see a part of it? I've seen that kind of exclusivity and I don't think it fits well with higher education."

It felt like Joe was in the room with me as I thought about how to answer each new question. "Each person is here for a reason," I continued. "Everyone's gifts need to be nurtured and shared like art. There's so much good to do, but we can't do it if we don't invite everyone."

The room got quiet again until Kelly broke the silence. "How does diversity show up in your life, Marcos?"

I paused as I thought about her question. "The Perez family is a diverse one. My parents and my brother are conservative Christians. My kids are little progressive lefties," I said with a proud smile. "One of them is trans. But we make it all work. How we make it work is what I was thinking about. It's love. Love provides a safe space for diversity to exist. We love each other and that allows us to stretch to fit each other's different perspectives. And in the end, we all end up with a broader understanding of things."

Cassie jumped in with the next question. "Naropa is about service to our community. In what way do you serve your community?"

"For most of my life, I've thought that my passion for art would give me meaning. But that changed this year when I followed my heart and did the next good thing in my community. I answered an ad in our neighborhood to help an old man with his daily needs. I had no experience at providing home care and had no way of knowing what would become of it. When I first saw him, he was twisted and stooped by a stroke—he looked so small and helpless. But after I worked with him and got to know him, I saw that he has so much wisdom and joy, and he's a light for so many. He is the person who showed me that people can be precious works of art. I did the next good thing as a service to my community, but I ended up learning about service from what I see him do in other people's lives every day," I concluded and took in a deep breath to weigh down the emotion rising in me. "That's a long answer, but the power of service to others has been a powerful lesson for me."

I looked over and each person remained motionless as though contemplating my words. Stillness and quiet were comfortable companions in this place.

"What is his name?" David asked.

"Joe," I answered with a smile as I rested my hand on the journal that contained so many of his lessons. "His name is Joe Sabah."

"Thank you for sharing, Marcos. That's wonderful and very much in line with our culture," Kelly offered. "The next question is: why do you want to work here?"

Why am I here? I thought and smiled inside. *I'm ready this time.* "Over my career, I've built brands, created messages, and imagined ads for products I never cared about: minivans, cowboy boots, investment banks, expensive jewelry. But Naropa seems to represent things that I love: poetry, art, dance, music, meditation, spiritual growth, expanding consciousness. I want those things for myself, and I can see myself helping others find their way here through creative work. That would be very meaningful," I said, starting to tear up again. "Sorry about that," I joked. "Some people cry during movies; apparently I cry during interviews."

"That's okay," Kelly replied. "Crying at interviews is very Naropa. Do you have any questions for us?"

I took another deep, calming breath as I imagined what Joe would do. "I told you why *I* am here. Why are each of *you* here?"

The room got quiet again for a few seconds as everyone smiled at each other. I could feel the emotion building until Cassie spoke. "I am free to be exactly who I am here. If I need to dance through the office to lift my spirits, nobody cares."

I looked over at David.

"I didn't know who I was when I came here. But this place is special. It allows me room to grow in ways that I would never have thought of. I'm never leaving, so I guess you're all stuck with me," David said, breaking into contagious tears.

Sam from the web team reached over and took his hand. "Naropa isn't perfect, but most days it's pretty close. I have to work in a place that values diversity."

Kelly spoke up last. "Oh, god. I may cry a little too. I need to be here because how else would I get to work with all my friends."

"That's probably a good point to conclude the interview," Cassie chimed in.

"Yes," Kelly said, wiping at her tears and smiling brightly again as she stood up and shook my hand. "It's great to meet you, Marcos. Let me walk you out."

We walked out and stood under the sycamores for a second. "I feel like I need to hug you," Kelly announced. "Is that okay?"

I opened my arms toward her. "I feel the same way. This was great," I said as she embraced me.

"I'll call you in a few days to follow up."

"Sounds good, Kelly. Talk to you soon."

Driving back to Denver, I was in a dreamlike mood. I couldn't imagine how my answers during the interview could have gone any better. I had asked to be there, had prepared for each question, and was proud of each response. I thought about picking up a rider on the way back, but I just wanted to stay in what felt like a thankful moment. Driving past my exit, I decided to go directly to Joe's to start on his daily chores. It was one hour until lunchtime. The phone rang when I was four blocks from Joe's apartment. It was Kelly.

"Hello, Marcos. I know I said I would call you in a few days, but we've been talking about you since you left, and we all agree that you are the best candidate and the best fit for Naropa. We'd like to make you an offer."

I buzzed with excitement as I rode the elevator up to Joe's floor. His door was cracked open as usual and I let myself in. Joe was at his computer and looked over his shoulder at me.

"Wow, look at you—a bow tie and everything. You're quite the dandy today," Joe said, turning to face me as I made my way over to him. "And by the look of that grin, I would say that your interview went pretty well."

I walked up to him and took his hand. "I got it!" I exclaimed. "They made me an offer less than an hour after the interview."

"Tell me about it," Joe said, holding my hand as I sat down on a chair next to him.

I recapped how our practice sessions had set me up for success, how I had complimented them, opened with a starting action, and showed how our cultures aligned. "They were all so nice. The head of the department even hugged me at the end."

"I had a great feeling about that place," Joe said.

"Joe, at the end of the interview, I looked around the conference room table and I asked them why *they* were here."

"Hey, that's *my* line." He squeezed my hand in anticipation. "Well?"

"Well, it was amazing. They all love the place so much that they got emotional describing why they are at Naropa."

"Excellent. It sounds like your kind of place, Marcos."

"They have the tuition benefit I was telling you about. Some of my co-workers—wow, I haven't said that in a while—some of them are taking classes and working toward a master's degree the same way I want to. They said the school is flexible about work schedules to allow employees to attend classes."

"You seem like a new man, Marcos."

Holding his hand and looking into his eyes, I felt like a new man. *I would have a paycheck next month, just in time to avert the foreclosure process. I would have health insurance for myself and the kids. I would have food in the house.* "This has saved me, Joe."

"Take a deep breath," Joe instructed.

I took a deep breath and let out a sigh of relief.

Joe got a serious look on his face. "Did you feel that? What is that?"

"It's a relief," I said, but I could tell he was looking for another answer. "I feel lighter, like how I told you I felt after the walk back from the concert." But that answer didn't satisfy him either and he kept his watery eyes locked on mine.

"You asked for this, didn't you, Marcos?"

I understood what he meant. I took another deep breath, and my heart was filled with gratitude. Pausing for a moment, I thanked the universe for honoring and answering my request. "I feel grateful. Thank you, Joe, for all your help and encouragement."

Joe dropped my hand and pointed upward as he smiled. I pointed up with him. "Thank you."

After a moment of silence, Joe looked over at me. "Well, it looks like it's time for *me* to ask for help."

He put his hand on his chest and closed his eyes. "Thanks for the answered prayer of Marcos. Thank you for bringing him to me, for our productive time together, and for our friendship, but now I need my next helper. Amen."

"Amen," I repeated, but must have given him a quizzical look.

"What, you don't think *you* could be the answer to someone's prayer? You are, Marcos, in more ways than one."

It was then that it hit me that my time with Joe was over.

"Okay then," Joe said matter-of-factly. "How long do I have you?"

"I start in a week and a half."

Joe reached up and circled the date on his wall calendar. "We'll have to get that 'Help Our Friend Joe' ad up and running again. Let's work on that after lunch. I think we should go out and celebrate."

I thought about what the next two weeks would be like for me, and for him. "I feel bad for leaving you, Joe."

"Don't do that. I'm going to be okay. I get to this stage with all my caregivers. I have them for a season and then it's 'Next!' and God brings me a new assignment—I mean helper," Joe said with a sly smile. "What is important is for you to start your new adventure and discover how it will help you to sing the song you came here to sing."

I thought about it as I sat with him. I knew that Naropa was the answer I had asked for. "I know that I need to be there as clearly as I knew that I needed to be with you."

Joe smiled and slapped his knee. "That's all I need to hear."

Lilly was in the living room when I got home. She glanced over at me and then did a double take. "Nice bow tie. I haven't seen you wear one in a long time. Oh, wait, you interviewed today." She turned to side-eye me. "Did you get it?"

I nodded slowly. "I got it. They offered me the job before I even got back from Boulder. Everyone is so nice. I think I'm going to like it there. Who knows, maybe I can finally stop worrying so much."

"Dad, that's great. When do you start? Tomorrow?" she prompted with a thumb motion toward the door.

"What? Are you that eager to get rid of me?"

"Nah," she quipped. "I just want everything to get back to normal for us."

"Me too, kiddo. We're on our way now. Where's Elliott? I want to tell him."

"He's been in his room all day. I think he's sleeping. You should text him about it, maybe that will get him up and going."

I sent him a text message and then went downstairs to review our finances. I started the laptop, checked my bank and Uber balances, and then looked at the calendar to count down the days until the first paycheck would hit. I would still be working for Joe until the last Friday, and I could still drive at night. That could get us through, and then I could just drive on the weekends until we were caught up on all the overdue bills. *We are going to make it*, I thought as I heard Elliott coming down the stairs.

"Hey, man, did you get my text message?" I shouted over my shoulder. "I'm so psyched to start my new job. I've already been thinking of some designs for them. I'll show you later tonight after I draft them."

He sheepishly walked over holding a red-stained washcloth on his upper thigh. "Dad, I think I have to go to the emergency room," he said as if apologizing.

I couldn't believe what I was hearing. "What are you talking about? What happened?"

"I cut myself again. It's deep this time. I think I need stitches or something. It won't stop bleeding."

I turned my chair around to face him, but my mind couldn't process what he was saying. "What did you cut yourself on?" And then it hit me. *He'd cut himself again, harming himself to cope with whatever was going on in his life.* I swallowed hard against the anger quickly rising in me and to steel myself for what I might see when he took the rag away. "Let me see it."

He pulled his hand away to reveal a long crimson slit that quickly filled with red to cover the white tissues exposed deep beneath. The sight overwhelmed me, and I had to turn away as my stomach dropped. It would need stitches if not something more. He covered the bloody wound and my mind immediately flashed to what the ER bill would be—five thousand? Ten? That wonderful feeling that everything was going to be okay left me in that moment and anger rushed into its place at being robbed of this first small victory. I was mad at God, mad at Elliott, but also mad at myself for not seeing this coming. I tried to keep it together, but my feelings just poured out through the open wound in my confidence. "Goddamn it, Elliott! Why do you do this to yourself? I'm trying so hard to pay for everything for us and all you can contribute is to carve yourself up? Do you have any idea how much an ER visit costs?"

"I'm really sorry, Dad," he sobbed. "I didn't mean for it to be so deep, but that's just how I feel about myself. I'm not okay right now."

"Go slip some shoes on," I ordered as I grabbed my phone and dialed my ex-wife.

I knew I should embrace him and be understanding, but it felt like he had cut us both and part of me just wanted to protect

229

myself from him. He could hurt himself, even end himself, at any moment and he felt like a time bomb in my house—ready to go off and destroy everything by taking away my son forever and leaving a pain that never goes away. I could feel the strong gravity from my fear at that moment but was powerless against its pull.

Lilly heard me yelling at the top of the stairs as I dialed Ursula a second time, only to go to voicemail again. "Damn it, I can't believe I have to deal with this crap today!" I didn't see Lilly behind me, and I released my frustration and fresh fear by punching the doorframe to the kitchen and letting fly a new series of curses.

"What the hell are you doing?" she shouted from behind me.

I turned to see a look of shock and horror on her face as if my daughter didn't recognize me. "Dad! Chill out!"

That was enough to snap me out of it. I told her what was happening, and she grabbed her bag just as Ursula called me back.

"Elliott cut himself again, and it's bad this time," I said to her between breaths. "We have to go to the ER."

"Again? Is he okay?"

"Yes, it's not life-threatening, but it will need stitches—it's deep. I have no idea where to take him."

"Drive over and pick me up. I will find an ER for us."

Lilly helped me line the back seat with an old towel before easing Elliott in. We stopped to pick up Ursula and she climbed into the back seat next to him. She was really sweet with him, but I was still fuming up front. *There's no way to trust this kid. There's nothing I can do to stop him. I can't take this anymore.* I tried to

remember Joe's lessons about fear taking the spotlight with everything moving around it, but I just wanted to feel safe again and it
felt like Elliott was preventing that. I could see that my fear was
like a trap, but I couldn't get out of it.

We pulled up to the emergency room entrance and Ursula led
Elliott inside. I parked the car and felt the awkward silence from
Lilly in the passenger seat. They admitted him and started closing up his cut, but when they learned it was from self-harm, they
ordered a mental health worker to interview him.

My stomach was killing me, and I thought I would be sick
while we waited. Ursula wanted to stay with him, and she suggested I drive Lilly home and stay there. *Was I still that visibly
angry? Did she want me away from this right now?* I wanted to be
away from this and lie down, so I agreed, and Lilly and I shared
a silent ride home.

Ursula called two hours later and said that Elliott was not safe
to come home. During his interview with the evaluator, Elliott
confessed that he had taken a handful of his medication earlier in
the day in hopes that it would kill him.

. . . and we're falling again. Everything just crashed for me
as I listened to her. Then it hit me how selfish I had been. I wanted
to drive right back to the ER to apologize, to love him, to hug him,
but they had already taken him away by ambulance and committed him to a mental health hold. Ursula was crying. I was crying. I
offered to come and get her, but she said that she had a ride coming for her. I don't think she wanted to be around me, and I didn't
blame her. She ended the call by saying that we could visit him for
fifteen minutes tomorrow and that I needed to bring his pajamas. I

knew that he would want art supplies, but she said the only things allowed were crayons and loose paper.

I ended the call and then crept down to my office, where I searched for the best quality water-based crayons I had and then fell into crying for my son.

CHAPTER 14

I lay awake most of the night wondering if my son was sleeping, wondering if they had sedated him, wondering if they were monitoring him. I got up and walked down the narrow hall to his door, but I paused as I touched the frame. Lilly said he had been sleeping most of the day, *but had he been unconscious from his attempted overdose?* I turned the handle and lingered in the open doorway. Moonlight fell on the hardwood floor, illuminating his empty, messed-up bed. I could have opened this door yesterday and found him motionless and unresponsive, already gone. A part of my heart died even to consider how close his end might have been. *What if he had taken more? What if he had taken something else? Is there any way I can protect him?*

Lying down in his bed, I recognized his scent but was overwhelmed with the thought that this smell could have been all that remained of him. I would have traded everything to be able to hold him right then, to feel him safe in my arms, to know he was okay.

My mind flashed back to my reaction at seeing him holding that bloody rag against his leg. My anger and frustration felt so misplaced now. I'd been working menial jobs, working at night, doing whatever it took to keep us afloat—and Joe had been a godsend to me—but being in his affirming company was such a different experience than what I felt looking up from my son's empty bed. I felt the weight of being a dad to an absent son, and I knew I was failing in ways I couldn't see. *What more could I be doing? What other guidance could I be offering? What other ways could I be loving him?* I replayed as I looked at the branches swaying in the night breeze.

Working with Joe had pulled me out of my depression and turned me around. Joe's lessons and coaching helped me get this new job, but were there other lessons I needed from him to help me with Elliott? And now I had less than two weeks left with him.

I got up with the sunrise and put on a pot of coffee to share with Lilly as I readied an institution-safe art kit for Elliott and waited until it was time to leave for our fifteen-minute morning visit.

Lilly was quiet and distant in the car. I tried talking to her about what I had put together for Elliott and what we should do when he got home.

"How are you doing?" I asked in another attempt to get through to her.

"I'm okay," she offered. "It's just Elliott." She looked down at her phone as I drove.

"He's getting the help he needs. He's going to be okay," I affirmed, hoping it was true.

She sat in silence and went back to the comfort of her phone screen.

"I don't know how to parent Elliott," I blurted out, unable to contain how afraid I felt. "How do you parent a kid who wants to die?"

Lilly looked up from her texts and let out a long sigh. "Dad, I don't know either. You're the parent, I'm just a kid."

I turned to look at her and felt the weight of her gaze as she looked over at me.

"One thing I do know is that you can't freak out like you did. One hundred percent not cool," she said, turning to face forward again.

"Yes, you're right. I've just been under so much pressure to keep it all together for us," I defended.

She sat looking straight ahead. I couldn't tell if she was about to yell at me or cry. "You know, you're not the only one who's suffering. He's my brother. I've seen it all. I want him to live too."

I realized how much I had been focusing on myself as I pulled into the hospital parking garage. My daughter was sitting right beside me, needing me, and I was missing it. "I'm sorry, honey. I can see this is hard on you."

Lilly looked over at me with an expression I couldn't read. "I just want to see Elliott. We should go," she said as she opened the car door.

Had I been working on the wrong things all this time? I wondered as I thought about which job I should be focusing on.

We were led into a small white meeting room with a wooden table and four chairs. A coffeemaker, cups, and tea bags sat atop a small wooden cabinet in the corner. Lilly got a coffee, and I made tea for me and Elliott while we waited.

He came in wearing green hospital scrubs, his sweatshirt from yesterday, and white no-skid socks with white rubber dots on the soles. Lilly went to him first and gave him a quick hug. I placed the teas down on the table and embraced him. I held him and lingered in that secure feeling that we were going to be okay.

Elliott returned my hug at first, then stiffened and pulled away. "I only have fifteen minutes," he said, moving to sit down. "Did you bring anything for me to wear?"

I pulled out three pairs of pajama bottoms and an assortment of vintage concert T-shirts and sweatshirts that Lilly had picked out. "We brought these," I said, pushing them toward him. "And I brought some art supplies for you. They have restrictions that we have to adhere to."

"I know," he acknowledged. "Crayons are allowed. Tell me you brought something better than crayons for me."

"Well, the rules are the rules—but I did find these nice water-color ones that should be a step up. And here is some nice folio paper," I said, offering them to him. Elliott smiled as we chatted for the remainder of our time, and I was careful to keep our talk to safe topics. It was a relief to see him, even in this sterile setting. *Could this be the bottom that we can all climb up from?*

I took Lilly back home but left as soon as I could to see Joe. We'd need to answer the "Help Our Friend Joe" replies and I just needed some Joe time. I had felt overwhelmed in my house and was overdue for some of his trademark sparkle.

I knocked and went in as Joe greeted me with a warm smile. "Marcos, come and sit with me. Did you celebrate your new job last night?"

I shook my head and told him about Elliott, my angry reaction, and how I had disappointed Lilly.

He listened patiently, nodded, and then smiled at me again. "I am sorry to hear that. But tell me, how is my friend Marcos doing?"

I smiled and chuckled nervously. I never needed Joe's guidance more than at this moment. "Why is life so hard?" I asked through the approaching tears.

Joe reached out and held my hand. "Life isn't hard, but it isn't easy either. It just is. It has down days and up days and they give each other meaning and show us the value of their lessons. Marcos, tell me what you are feeling right now."

I could feel the weight of the words in my throat. They were dark and felt like they had been there for a while. *Had I been afraid to voice them?* "One day Elliott is going to do it and there's nothing I can do to stop him. I can't talk him into loving his life. I thought if I just loved him enough, it would help me to go and find him in his dark spot on the map and lead him back to a brighter place, lead him back to loving his life. But we can't make anyone love anything, can we? I can't keep going like this, Joe. I keep thinking that I'll open his door and find him lifeless in his bed. I'm losing hope and I feel like I need to pull back from him and his darkness just to protect myself, but I know that isn't right."

"You're correct, Marcos. Pulling back isn't right. I can see you're in a dark place today, my friend," Joe said as he squeezed my hand and then bent over to kiss it sweetly. "My dear, dear Marcos. Did you look forward to coming over here this morning?"

237

"Yes," I blurted out, unable to control my emotions any longer. "More than anything. I just needed some Joe this morning."

"You wanted to come over here more than anything because you knew what you would find. You knew I would be my same joyful self, didn't you?"

I nodded.

"And you knew being with me would be exactly what you needed today, on this most difficult of days?"

"Yes, exactly. I needed an anchor of positivity to hang on to today."

Joe smiled at me with something that felt like pride. "Well, congratulations, my friend. You've just figured out your next good thing to do. Your next assignment is for *you* to be that anchor for the people in your life, like your son."

"Ha! Is that all?" I laughed through my tears. "Even on days like today?"

"Especially on days like today," Joe affirmed. "Do you remember me telling you that being positive isn't always easy?"

"I remember. You said some days it takes more effort than it looks like from the outside."

"And today is one of those days. It will feel like you want to pull back, but you can't. When you want to protect yourself, that's when you need to make yourself even more vulnerable. On days like today, being someone else's anchor of positivity will be the hardest thing you ever do—but it will also be the most important."

"Positive beats negative," I stated.

"Always," Joe emphasized. "Keeping your positive outlook is always the next good thing to do because you never know who's going to need it, or when."

I knew Joe was about to deliver an uncomfortable lesson.

"It's impossible to stop loving them, Marcos, no matter what they do. There is no pulling back or protecting yourself. We love our kids with all our hearts and that's it. You're kidding yourself if you think it could be any other way."

"You're right, Joe, but loving them is not protecting them," I challenged as I wiped at my eyes. "Something happened to me when I first held Elliott and Lilly after they were born. My heart made a promise not to let anything happen to them. But now, I'm realizing I can't protect them."

"You can't protect them from everything, but the *way* you love can protect them from a lot. Love them relentlessly. Every day is a new opportunity to practice loving them," Joe said, looking out the window for his next thought. "No matter what they do—you show up. If you disagree—show up and be positive. If they ignore you—show up anyway and love them. If they scare you—show up and be their anchor just like I was for you today."

He looked back at me and laughed. "Being a parent is a life sentence with no possibility of parole. You'd better get used to those stripes."

That made me laugh, and it felt good. *Who was I kidding? There was no protecting my heart.*

"Don't be afraid. Prepare yourself every morning to love them relentlessly. Ask for their happiness and joy in the same way

239

you asked for your own guidance and success. Do this in every moment of your day, when you're driving, when you're sipping tea, when you're strumming your ukulele. Wish them health, friendship, love, peace, and joy. And make sure to ask for it out loud when you ask. You've seen how that is key."

"Wishing doesn't make it happen for them, Joe."

Joe laughed out loud as though I'd missed the point entirely. "The wishes don't work directly on them; they work on *you*. They are to keep you focused on *your* mission should it get difficult— and it *will* get difficult. Not all songs are happy ones, Marcos. Some songs are dark. But you can't see only the darkness they present to you. In Elliott's case, you must look past what presents to the world and see him for the blessing he is. He is more than what he's showing you now; he isn't just trouble or a problem to fix. You have loved him his entire life. He is your beloved son. If you can't see that in him now when he is at his darkest, he will never be able to see that in himself. Don't you see how you are the key?"

I did. I let go of Joe's hand and placed it over my heart as I took in his words. "Please help me be the father my son and daughter need right now," I asked out loud just like I had done those times before. "Please strengthen me to be a positive light when it gets dark."

Joe sat silently until I opened my eyes. "The most powerful force in the universe is how we see the world. Master that and it will guide every action you need to take, Marcos. You will know what to do in the moment. Let your love guide you, not your fear."

"Thank you, Joe," I said, taking his hand again. "I knew talking to you would be just what I needed."

"Marcos, you can come by anytime—even after I get a new caregiver. Speaking of that, we have two responses already. Can you help me set up interviews with them?"

"Sure, Joe. Let's get that moving."

The hospital had put Elliott on a seventy-two-hour hold, but we were allowed to visit him for fifteen minutes on the second and third days, and I brought more clothes and art supplies for him.

The supervising psychologist coached us to keep the first conversations superficial and not to judge or talk about the events that had led up to the attempt. Elliott talked about how much he hated the no-skid socks they were forced to wear and how they had taken the drawstring out of the sweatshirt hoodie I brought him. I talked about Zuzu and Lilly talked about how dumb her classes were. I sketched out the designs I was planning for the start of my new job, and he was interested in going deeper into that.

The doctors kept us behind on the second day to review their recommended three-step home care protocols. Step one, buy a safe. Step two, search the house for anything dangerous to Elliott or anything that could even trigger thoughts of self-harm. Step three, put those things in the safe and get them for Elliott when needed. So we rounded up the kitchen knives, scissors, all his medications, all my medications, the car keys, all the sharp-edged tools from the garage, and even the X-Acto knives out of both of our art kits. "You're the first line of defense for keeping

Elliott alive," they told me. *Parental guidance I never expected to hear.*

On Elliott's release day, they presented us with his outpatient schedule. Two hours every day after school and four hours on Saturdays. They encouraged us to do family activities on Sunday and not to leave Elliott alone for more than an hour at a time. I asked about how we should interact with him or care for him and what we should discuss about his depression and the events that had led to his attempt. "This is the experience he's having right now," they said. "It's Elliott's recovery to own and work."

I was hoping for clearer direction from them on what I could do. In the end, I decided to take Joe's guidance to just show up, be positive, and love relentlessly at every opportunity. *I would be to Elliott what Joe had been to me.*

I went straight to Joe's after the three daily hospital visits, where I added home care screener and interviewer to my daily chores.

"I want you to answer every email response," Joe instructed. "No matter how weird they sound or how bad their spelling is. Some of my best caregivers' emails would have been immediately dismissed by anyone in their right mind."

"So what does that say about us then?" I asked.

"That's a good one," Joe laughed. "They *do* need to be on time, though. Punctuality is basic courtesy. And I can't be late to any of my doctor appointments because they charge you now."

"Must be on time. Got it," I said, remembering being on the other end of his emails. "Anything else?"

"No experience required."

"I'm proof of that."

"You'll train them just like Patrick trained you. Besides," Joe joked, "I know a thing or two about taking care of an old man by now."

The replies trickled in over the next few days: a retired nurse who had just moved to Denver to be near her daughter, a teacher who only taught night classes, and a warehouse worker who was unable to drive his forklift while recovering from an accident. I responded to every new email and set up interviews over lunch at Perkins or at Joe's apartment. One by one the candidates came, I asked them what background they had, if any, and Joe asked them why they were here. Joe got some answers, but apparently not the answer he was looking for as he thanked each one and said we'd be in touch.

After the last interviewee left our lunch table on the Wednesday of my last week, I was starting to get worried. "Joe, why didn't you go with Helen?" I asked. "She's perfect. She lives nearby, has worked with patient care before, and she's nice. Didn't you think she was nice?"

"Yes, she's nice," Joe hesitated. "She's just not what I'm looking for."

Not what you're looking for? I asked myself. *We're on a deadline here.* "What about Kenny from yesterday? He has three months before his next deployment, was very qualified, and he has a nice car."

"I considered him, but Patrick saw our email and forwarded it on to someone he thinks would be perfect. Marty is his name. We meet him tomorrow."

"Joe, I don't think you have time for perfect. I start my new job on Monday."

"Oh, I know. I have a feeling about this guy."

"A feeling?"

"Sure. Don't forget, I had a feeling about you, didn't I?" Joe said with a wry smile.

We sat down for lunch and started with just coffee until Joe's new candidate arrived. Joe kept an eye on the entrance as I prepared the two creams for his cup.

"Do you know what he looks like?" I asked.

"Patrick said he was middle-aged with dark hair and is thin. He described me to him, so he won't be able to miss the handsome man with a striking cane," Joe said as he patted his "chick magnet" walking stick.

"I'm going to miss you, Joe," I said, feeling a bit of sadness that our paths were parting.

"I think that's him," Joe prompted as he raised his hand and waved.

The man noticed Joe and came over to sit beside me as I scooted farther into the booth. "Are you Joe?"

"Yes, it's a pleasure to meet you, Marty," Joe said, extending his hand.

I introduced myself and studied him as he spoke. He looked to be a couple of years younger than me and was thin as a stick. The bags under his eyes made him look tired, but there was something deeper than exhaustion there. He seemed nervous and high-strung as he flagged down a server to get a coffee.

"I'm on a break from my job at the electronics store, so I'll need to get my lunch order in too, if that's okay. I mean, I won't have a job next week," he rambled. "I quit and tomorrow is my last day. It's been so stressful, a nightmare really. They have been letting people go and then adding me to more and more shifts. I have a new boss now. I was up for the position, but they wanted 'new blood.' The guy is ten years younger and is just running everyone into the ground. I was booked for fourteen days straight before I quit. Aah, here she is. I'd like a Reuben sandwich, please, and a Coke."

Joe took a slow sip of his coffee. "So why are you interested in helping me?"

Marty squirmed as he answered. "Patrick forwarded your 'Help Our Friend Joe' email and I guess I just need something different. I want to be doing something with my time, so I thought why not do this?"

"Have you ever done anything like home care before?" I asked as I started in on the standard interview questions I had prepared for all the candidates. Marty hadn't done anything close to home care, aside from helping his elderly parents now that he had moved back in with them after his divorce. He responded to each of my questions with a long-winded answer that usually ended by describing some personal hardship. He was the least qualified, and, by my assessment, the least capable candidate to date.

"So why are you here, Marty?" Joe asked over our lunch plates.

Marty repeated some of his sad stories and I could see where this was going as Joe set him up.

"No, Marty. Why are you here?" he asked, opening his arm wide.

"Oh, like why am I here on earth?" Marty asked as he dropped back into the booth—his body language relaxing for the first time. "God, good question. At this point, I don't think I know anymore. I tried being the family man and that blew up in my face. I thought I'd be a career man, but they passed me up. I'm out of work tomorrow. I'm burned-out. I'm not sleeping. I'm living with my parents again so that I can afford my child support, so kiss any love life goodbye. And I'm forty-five years old. Obviously, I suck at life."

The man beside me was clearly frustrated and becoming emotional as he shared details on setback after setback. I felt for him but quietly chuckled to myself at what I knew was going to happen next.

Joe looked over at me and then smiled at Marty. "Well, you sound perfect! Can you start on Saturday?"

"W-w-what?" Marty stammered. "But I just shared all that stuff about—"

"I said you're perfect, Marty," Joe interrupted. "You are perfect. And I want you to help me starting Saturday. How does that sound?"

Marty's shoulders slumped with what felt like relief at being valued when he clearly didn't value himself. "Yes, Joe. Just tell me when and where. I'm here for you."

"Meet us here tomorrow for lunch again and Marcos here will show you the ropes."

"Sure thing, Joe," Marty said, reaching for his wallet to pay his share of the bill.

Joe cut him off. "It's on me, my friend. I'm excited to work with you, Marty. You're going to be great."

* * *

The next day, we arrived at Perkins at our usual time and Marty was already there waiting for us.

"Hello, Marty," Joe said as we walked in. "Do you have time to have lunch with us again?"

"I have all the time we need," Marty replied. "They had a final check ready when I walked in the door. I'm done there. I don't have to go back, and I feel better already. So, when do we start?"

"That's great news. We start right now. Take my hand and walk me over to that booth," Joe said, letting go of my hand. "That's it. Now hold me steady as I stoop to sit down. You've got it. In no time you'll be as good as dance teacher Marcos here."

"Are you really a dance teacher?" Marty asked as he slid into the booth next to me.

"I used to be. I'm a graphic designer, recently reemployed," I answered, taking a seat beside him. "I start my new job on Monday, so this is my last day with Joe."

"It's been wonderful," Joe said. "And it will be wonderful with you, Marty. Now let's get some lunch, I've got two hungry men to feed today."

"Mayor of Perkins? What does that mean?" Marty asked me, pointing to the name tag I'd pinned on Joe before we left.

"You'll see," I said, chuckling at what was in store for him. "He's a mini celebrity wherever he goes."

Joe asked Steve, the restaurant manager, if we could have Twyla as our server for my last day. She greeted Marty, said goodbye to me, and chatted with Joe as usual. Soon other servers and Perkins lunch regulars stopped by Joe's booth to meet the new caregiver and to thank me for my time with Joe. We barely had time to finish our lunches between all the conversations. Joe beamed and drank it all in while Marty just smiled and shook his head in wonder.

Joe paid the bill after the last regulars had left and Marty followed us back to Joe's apartment, where I showed him the daily chores just like Patrick had shown me. Marty didn't mind any of it and he seemed to be happy doing anything other than the old job that he still complained about. He stuck around for a cup of tea before heading to the bank to deposit his final check.

"I told you I had a feeling about Marty," Joe said to me.

I nodded. "Yes, I think he'll do great for you. And I'm sure that you're exactly what he needs right now. A pat on the head and a thumb in the back."

Joe laughed. "Poor guy. Seems like he needs one of everything."

"I see what you were looking for now," I said, giving him a long look.

"Knowing what to look for is the first step in helping," Joe said. "How are things going with your son?"

"They approved his release a few days ago. He's home with us now. We think we have his medication right. He seems happier and more engaged. They gave us some things to do to protect him, but I am following your advice going forward: relentless love, showing up at every opportunity, bringing him to a better place on the map, asking for his joy, being positive. I aim to be for him what you were for me."

"What have I been for you?"

I laughed at the thought that he didn't know. "You were an answer to a desperate request when I was at a dark point and couldn't see a way forward. You showed me a path out of where I was. And now that I'm on it, I see how I can show it to others like Elliott. You showed me how to be. I watched how you move through the world. I saw how you carefully create and protect a positive space for everyone around you to thrive in," I said, holding in the tears that I felt rising. "I would say that I will miss that feeling, but I won't. I know I can create it myself now, so I think I'll keep it."

"You just described my song."

"I wrote down parts of it too," I said, patting my leather bag that contained my journal.

"That's good. You still owe me that assignment of getting your writing out there," Joe chuckled.

I smiled and nodded.

"I have one final lesson for you, Marcos. The Bible says, 'give us our daily bread.' But at eighty-seven, I say, Lord, give me my daily day. Every morning that I open my eyes is another day that I get to sing my song. I sing about how wonderful life is and how lucky we are to be here. I sing it as bravely as I can now. I sing it so that others can hear and join in. I treat each new daily day as a fresh opportunity to be a positive example and to help everyone around me. Being positive is powerful. Every day my body gets weaker, and I don't work the way I used to," he said, moving his twisted left arm. "But with positivity and the anticipation of helping others, I am more than enough to do all the good I can with each new day. So the final lesson is to treat each new day as a challenge for how much good *you* can do. This is what I want for you. Use what you've learned from me when you are at Naropa, when you are driving people around, when you are with your kids. Don't miss *any* opportunity. Do it daily. You have so much good to do, Marcos."

He smiled and held up his thumb in approval, but then turned it sideways and pushed it at me like a prod. "Now get out there!"

And just like that, I knew my time with this teacher was over. I couldn't help but laugh. "The old thumb in the back!"

I got up, hugged him, and told him that I loved him. He looked at me and nodded, his voice cracking with emotion as his eyes welled up. "You're going to be great."

CHAPTER 15

I quickly fell in love with peaceful, contemplative, and quirky Naropa. I had the best cubicle in the department. It opened in the back to a large window that framed the most beautiful tree on campus. I had the view all to myself, but quickly realized an empty chair would attract others—so I placed one behind my cube next to the window and it became effective conversation bait to get to know everyone there. People would come by and take a break in my extra chair and start talking about a project they were stuck on or just come by and see what I was sketching. Some would just come and relax in my chair and look at my beautiful tree in silence while they recharged.

My new job was a great place for deep conversation as most of my co-workers were active in some kind of contemplative practice such as meditation, yoga, or philosophy. I loved these deep and meaningful conversations as they gave me ample opportunities to use Joe's lessons with others. I would be engrossed in my work and would suddenly hear someone flop into my chair with a heavy sigh and I knew it was time to give them a big Joe smile and create a bubble of positive love around them.

Using Joe's lessons almost daily also kept them at the top of my mind for being the dad Elliott needed. He was improving with new meds and daily outpatient therapy after class, but I felt like my showing up, being positive at every interaction, and loving him relentlessly, even on days when it felt unwanted, was helping to keep him in a good place. I would drive from work to pick him up from therapy and we would both talk about our day's deep conversations.

One of my frequent bubble flyers was Cassie, the writer and assistant art director from my interview. She had been a professional ballet dancer and looked like she could spring into a dance step from any posture. Cassie even wrote like a dancer: flowing, artistic, and on point. A common topic between us was fathoming the mysteries of the magic that Naropa had, but that everyone struggled to pin down. If I asked, "What is Naropa?" people would describe it differently, but if different people would describe something as "so Naropa," everyone would know what they meant.

Cassie flopped down in my chair one Friday afternoon, and when I turned around, her posture looked weighted, and her energy felt smaller somehow. I smiled as wide as I could as I imagined my friend Joe sitting with us. "Hey, what's up?"

I could tell she was troubled and was holding something inside that needed to come out. She looked out at the tree for a few seconds and asked, "Marcos, why are men idiots?"

I just laughed. "Present company excluded I hope."

She joined in with a chuckle that slipped into a smile. "It has to be me."

"What has to be you?"

"I keep picking the same guy. That guy who is super creative, loves me to bits, and then just pulls back as soon as I am interested. Am I supposed to play hard to get?" she asked as she shifted in the chair for what felt like it would be a long conversation. "Why should I have to *play* at anything? I just want a life with someone, is that crazy?"

I smiled at her and settled in. "It's beautiful to want to share a life. Don't hide your desire for that. It sounds like these guys want to be with you, but they run out of maturity when it gets serious. They may try to spin up some drama to keep hanging on, but they lost you when you showed up as an adult."

"What the heck," she said, slumping in the chair with a sigh. "How do you tell the men from the boys?"

"Look for the ones who can keep up."

"What do you mean?"

"Cassie, I've seen you lead big projects, manage every detail, put out fires, and generally kick butt. It's impressive," I said, blowing over my hot tea. "You are a dynamic and powerful woman, don't hide from that fact. Show up like that—the men will love it, the boys will run out of steam and quit."

She sat back up in her chair. "And then what?"

I felt like Joe was right next to me in my cube and now was my time to channel him. "I have a magic word for you: *Next.*"

"Next?"

"Raise your hand like you are about to wave goodbye," I said as I raised my hand, and she copied me. "Now say the magic word." I started waving goodbye as she said the word *next*.

She laughed. "That's great, but my arm's going to get tired."

"It might, but one day you'll meet one who doesn't quit. Keep looking forward. He's out there. You will know him by the way he says yes to you. His yeses will be followed by the word *and*."

She seemed to brighten as she pondered Joe's words. "Yes!" she exclaimed. ". . . *and* I love it."

"What do you want? You're a dancer—imagine your dream life as a song. What are the lyrics, what is the rhythm? How does it go, Cassie?"

"I want a house and five kids," she replied without hesitation.

"That's very specific."

"Oh, and a big fluffy dog that they all play with."

"There is a guy out there who will say yes to that. Just keep hitting the next button until you find him."

"Do you really think so?" she wondered as though asking for permission to keep hoping.

"Do you ask to meet him?"

"Ask? Ask who?" she said with a confused look.

"The universe, God, a higher power, whatever you believe in. I know it sounds weird but trust me, it works if you ask out loud," I said, standing up. "Come on, let's go for a walk outside and I'll show you."

David, the multimedia specialist from my interview, was another regular visitor to my cube. "Where's my chair?" he'd ask if I'd left my coat or my canvas backpack sitting in *his* chair. He was hired as the videographer, photographer, and archivist, but I could tell his passion was the Naropa podcast

254

he'd started and which had grown to be a major outreach tool for the university.

He plopped down in his chair on a Friday morning, and I could immediately tell he was upset. "What's up?" I asked.

"I thought you should hear it from me first. I've started applying for other jobs," David blurted out. "And they pay like twenty thousand more than Naropa. Marcos, my friend, I am being truly undervalued here."

I grabbed my tea and then turned to give David my full attention. "Well, that's not how it looks to me. I, for one, value you tremendously. I have worked with a lot of videographers in my career. Your eye is great. I can feel the emotion in your work. I have seen a lot of people botch the audio with their vids, but yours is always flawless."

"Thanks for that," David conceded with a shy smile. "We are a Buddhist university. Have you ever heard the term 'Right Livelihood'?"

I shook my head and welcomed my next Buddhist lesson.

"It says that the way you support yourself is an expression of your deepest self."

"And your 'deepest self' doesn't want to struggle to pay the rent?" I said with a satisfied smile, knowing that Joe would have loved that setup question.

David leaned in with a laugh. "No, it does not."

"Meaning is often more important than money," I offered as I scooted closer to him. "I used to make more money than I do now, but that work didn't hold any meaning for me. It was hollow. But this place is different. When we first met, you said this place

255

allowed you to grow in ways you couldn't imagine and that you'd never leave. It feels like you are on a different spot on the map right now. Why is that?"

"I don't know," David hesitated. "I still love this place and I treasure it, but that extra money would be meaningful to me right now."

"But what could you be walking away from?" I challenged. "I learned a valuable lesson this year about perspective, about recognizing where you are and where you wish you could be. You know when you go into the mall, there is a map near each entrance with a big red dot that says, 'You are here.' You may be where you want to be at that moment, or you might want to be somewhere else, and you have to walk to another spot. But our minds work differently. They don't have to walk—we can just pick the red dot we're on and move it to where we want, and we can do this anytime we want. But if we're not careful, our minds can wander away from the space we wanted to stay on to somewhere that looks more attractive but might not be. Question for you: if you were standing on another spot with an extra twenty thousand a year, could it purchase what you might miss from here?"

David turned in his chair and looked out at the tree. "That sounds like a valuable lesson."

"It's empowering when you realize that *you* get to choose where you are on the map."

"I suppose I need to choose carefully."

"What are you most excited about doing here? Is it the video, the new podcast, gleaning the old footage for nuggets?"

"It's the podcast," he said, brightening. "I just know it can be huge for us."

"I think it can be too," I answered, knowing I was onto something for him. "I heard from Kelly that it is one of the fastest-growing academic-focused podcasts in the country."

"She said that?"

"She did. It's you, David," I affirmed. "You're like the voice of Naropa right now."

"Well, I don't know about that."

"Sure, if not you, then who? You are so skilled at interviewing, and you bring such genuine curiosity and excitement to your topics that it creates this really exciting space that brings out the best in people. Just keep doing that. Sometimes we just need to give for a while before we get anything back. Lean into that passion and I know something good will happen from it."

I drove straight from work to pick up Elliott from therapy. Three other kids around Elliott's age waited next to him for their rides.

He flopped into the car seat with a sigh. "Thanks for coming to get me."

I could tell that he was exhausted. *Was he tired from therapy or from something else that he was dealing with?* "It's good to see you. How's it going?"

He shrugged and plugged his phone into the car stereo's auxiliary cord. "Do you mind if I put something on?"

"Sure, why don't you DJ for a while."

The light of his phone lit up his face as he searched. "Hmm, maybe. Nope," Elliott said as he considered selections and then rejected them. "I can't do Crywank right now. Oh, you like Mother Mother—'Ghosting' seems appropriate right now."

I steered us onto the highway as the song started. "What do you mean?"

Elliott sat up in his seat. "I've decided that I just need to ghost those guys at school. It's time to let all that stuff go from my old group. Those relationships aren't serving me. I'm ready for what's next."

Wow, I thought to myself. *He's already using the Next advice. What other breakthroughs is he having?* "That sounds really healthy. How are you doing with that?"

"I'm not going to lie, I hate it. Sometimes I'm still angry about it; other times it hurts. More often, like now, I just feel numb to it."

258

"Is that okay, to feel numb?"

"It's just an emotion," Elliott answered in a voice filled with newfound confidence. "I have a lot of them. They come and go, but I don't judge them anymore. I decide how much attention they get and what to do about them."

That sounds like the right spot on the map, I thought as I took our exit. "Well, you sound like you're in a better place with everything. Unfortunately, lived wisdom is usually the hardest wisdom to come by, but you are doing it. I am impressed with you, kid."

"And now I have the scars to prove it," he laughed. "I don't know if I am in a good place or not, but this is who I am at this moment. I know now that I'm not responsible for the problem, but

THE NEXT GOOD THING

I *am* responsible for the solution to it. I'm learning that I have a lot of work to do."

Could it be this easy? Just point to what he is doing well and create a positive space for it to grow? "I'm proud of you, son. Let me know how I can help."

"Honestly, Dad, you've been really great. Just keep loving me like this."

Things were going well at the new job. Kelly and the team loved my work and I felt like a core member of their creative family as I took on more and more creative tasks. More new people kept sitting in my chair to look at my tree and spend some time in the Joe-like environment I tried to create every day. My cubicle became a place where people gathered to charge up or to unload a burden that was slowing them down. I tried to envision my old friend sitting in the chair when it wasn't occupied by my new friends. Thinking about him there would immediately make me smile. *Would he be proud of my progress?*

I watched through my window as the autumn light grayed and the leaves on my tree turned and then fell before winter settled in. On a snowy morning in December, I had just grabbed a coffee and said my hellos to the rest of the team, when I opened my email and saw the subject line I had been dreading: "Remembering Joe Sabah, 1931–2019."

"Oh no," I said out loud. My heart sank as I read the email from Judy that "Joe had made his transition" after struggling with pneumonia.

259

Danny, one of my new friends at work, stuck her head around the corner of my cubicle. "Is everything okay, Marcos?"

"My friend Joe just died," I said, tearing up.

"Oh no," Danny said, moving over to sit in the empty chair. "I'm sorry to hear that. Was he young?"

"No," I said, shaking my head. "He just turned eighty-eight not too long ago. He was a mentor to me and helped me through a really difficult time in my life."

"Do you feel like talking about it?" she asked.

I did. I felt like telling the world about what he had done for me. "Before I came to work here, I was his home care provider. He had suffered a stroke a few years before, so he needed help to do some things, but he ended up helping me much more than I helped him."

"He sounds amazing," Cassie said, peeking her head around the other cubicle wall.

"He was amazing," I said. David, Kelly, and others came to my cube as I described our time together. "He was at the end of his life, half paralyzed, and struggled with basic things, but he was never down or depressed or anxious about anything. He stepped up every day with an unflinching positive attitude that just fueled him to do as much good as he could with his life. He was an inspiration."

"I totally want to be like that when I'm older," Danny said.

"When was the last time you saw him?" Kelly asked.

"I saw him on his birthday, but I could have stopped by so many other times," I conceded with regret. "I don't know why I didn't."

"We have to love them while we have them with us," Cassie said.

What more should I have said to him? What other ways could I have cared for him? "There's something I owed him but never did," I added. "He gave me an assignment to write about our time together. I drafted it once, but I lost it and never went back to it. I think that disappointed him. I wish I could have given him that when I had the chance."

"Maybe you could do it now," Danny prompted. "Like a eulogy of sorts. It might give you some closure and make you feel better."

I nodded and mustered a smile. "Maybe."

CHAPTER 16

The white computer screen illuminated the basement as I thought about what I could use as a starting point to describe Joe Sabah. *Would it be Joe's laugh? Would it be leading him as we walked? Would it be the wisdom and love that motivated so many?*

Joe had been on my mind since I first got the email about his death, and I wished more than anything that I had gone to see him again. *Surely I could have spared an hour or two to see him just once more*, I thought as I wiped at the tears rising in my eyes. I pulled the photograph of Joe and me with the ukulele out of my desk drawer and placed the image below the monitor as I thought about how I could describe my journey with him. No one in Joe's family had asked me to prepare a eulogy, but I knew that I needed to do it. I owed it to him. I was eager to share the gift that Joe had given me, but I also feared that this amazing man might pass from the world without notice. I looked down at our faces in the photograph and resolved to sit at the computer into the night until the right words came.

Writing about myself felt weird, but there was no way of telling his story without telling my own. I imagined telling my story with Joe in front of his friends and family at the memorial service and it made me feel like hiding.

Hiding, I thought as my fingers hovered over the keyboard. "Don't hide." Joe's words came back to me as I reached for the drawer that contained the old journal I had put away after getting the job at Naropa. Opening the worn book, I knew I would find a nugget of wisdom from Joe about not hiding at a moment like this. "Don't hide" was highlighted in yellow as "Lesson #2" in my hand-written notes from our time together. I flipped through the journal and when I found nine other Sabah lessons that I had highlighted, I knew I had found my way to memorialize my old friend. Joe's thin voice sparkled in my mind as I began typing about each one:

1. Find Your Song: Each of us has a unique gift to share with the world—this is our song, and we are fulfilled when we sing it for others.

"I can hear you singing," I remembered him saying as I held the pages of the journal open in front of the keyboard. *Is fulfillment the way to know that you are singing the song you came here to sing?* I wondered.

I read the journal passage again and the words "share with the world" and "sing it for others" jumped out at me. I had shared my art through my new job, and it felt rewarding. I had shared myself with my new son and had protected him on his journey to becoming a man. Isn't that fulfillment?

2. Don't Hide: *You* are the gift the world needs. Embrace the gift as your song and sing it loudly.

"Why are you hiding, Marcos?" was the first challenge that Joe had used to knock me out of my comfortable darkness. My laughter filled the basement as I recalled the panic I'd felt about Joe threatening to send the "Ukulele Magic" email to his entire coaching list. It wasn't Joe's subtlest lesson, but it taught me that I could no longer use expected roles or comfort zones to hide from who I am.

What a gift Joe had to be able to see the potential in others that they could not see in themselves. He saw mine, and he helped me see Elliott's. *How many others out there need to stop hiding?*

3. It's That Easy: Point to what people are doing right and they will change to that frequency in their lives.

Joe made it look easy, and then he showed me how it could be almost effortless—with daily use. *How many times had I used this with Elliott, with Lilly, with random Uber passengers, with colleagues at work?* I could hear Joe's voice again, encouraging me to keep doing this to stay in practice.

4. You Get by Giving: "Having" is a two-sided coin made of giving and receiving.

My fingers stopped above the keys as I replayed his words. *Did I have this better life now because I had assisted him first?* I *had* given, but now those menial home care tasks seemed so small compared to what Joe had given back. *Could I ever repay it?*

5. Ask for Help: Ask a higher power, ask the universe, ask God, but ask out loud.

"It was right here," I said out loud. "It was from this very chair that I asked for it." I directed my voice toward the ceiling and the higher power that had once directed me to just do the next good thing.

"Thank you," I offered as I flipped to Joe's next lesson.

6. The Power of Next: Drop something that's not working and look forward with anticipation to better things ahead.

I can still picture Joe raising his right hand and waving goodbye to disappointment, hardship, anger, and loss like they were standing pedestrians shrinking in the rearview mirror of a car accelerating out of sight. Letting go was uncomfortable for me, but focusing my mind on what good awaited me in the future showed the power of Next.

7. You Are Here: Pick up your red spot on the map and move it to the neighborhood you want.

I smiled at the small drawing I had made of Joe's clipped Ziggy cartoon that he kept on the wall above his desk. "You are here*," it read with an asterisk above a red dot on a map, "but this sign isn't where it's supposed to be*." I had copied the cartoon into the margin on the journal page to remind me of how transformative it felt to pick up my spot and move into an area of empowerment. That was an important day when I knew I could choose a different future for myself and my family.

8. Positive Beats Negative: Stop *everything* to resist *anything* negative.

"The most powerful force in the universe is how we see the world," Joe said to me near the end of our time together. *How many times had I seen him light up a room, attract and win over complete strangers, or remain an anchor of hope and optimism that others could depend on when they drifted?* Now that I'm starting to see the world the way he did, I know he was right.

I laughed out loud when I read "Thumb in the back" underlined next to this lesson. Oh, how Joe made me uncomfortable sometimes, but he always knew the positive touch I needed to get over my excuses. "I'll give you a pat on the head or a thumb in the back to get you going"—I could hear his voice as if coaxing me on with this task for tomorrow. *How much good had this old man manifested in others just because he wouldn't tolerate their excuses?*

9. Happy People Have Happy Lives: Our choices drive our behavior—and our behavior defines our destiny.

We talked about destiny in a pharmacy parking lot. "Sad people lead sad lives," Joe said to snap me out of my negative behaviors, driven by a thousand bad choices in how I reacted to obstacles in my life. He made it look easy to make positive, loving, and reaffirming choices at every opportunity, but when I saw that even *he* had to be purposeful in his daily choices—that's when I knew that *anyone* could change, including me.

10. Our Daily Day: Treat each day as a new opportunity to do some good in the world.

The final lesson. "We have so much good to do today," Joe had said to me before we left for that first lunch together. I remembered thinking, *How can he be so sure?* But day after day, hand in hand, I saw his intention and his results. "Give us this day, our daily day" was his call to action for this final lesson that drew on the other nine. I thought back to our days together: *How satisfied would Joe have been with the good he had done at the end of each of his days?*

After finishing all ten lessons, I leaned back in the chair and reviewed what I had typed. Reading the words felt like looking back over a long bridge to a place of struggle. I let my mind drift back in time to the desperation that had felt so strong then and I found that old spot on the other side that marked the beginning of the story when I'd first read his name on the email: "Help Our Friend Joe."

I had listened to the guidance in this basement to do the next good thing. *I had helped Joe.* I helped him overcome his impairment, which had helped him to sing his song a little while longer.

I remembered Joe's laughter in my interview to be his caregiver. Joe laughed as though he knew I was a parting gift of yet another hopeless turnaround project that he could make into one more song for himself. *Was I his last song?* I wondered as the words of our story started to appear on the screen. If I was, then that only increased the importance of what I was writing. I focused on the sound of the clicking keyboard as I let the words spill out of my heart, words which I hoped would help others understand and appreciate the giant that lived inside that small, injured man.

I thought back to his thin voice, his stern motivating look, and his smile that brought out the goodness in people. I finished the first page as I remembered how it felt to be near him and see

267

him work his magic on others. I recalled the feeling of his weathered hand in mine as we walked, and it reminded me that Joe never walked from place to place—it was always from person to person. Words continued onto the second page as I flashed back to him slowing and ultimately stopping our strides whenever he saw a new opportunity to engage a stranger and bring one of these life lessons to them.

I stopped at the bottom of the second page and thought about the size of the gift Joe had given me. Joe had delivered it in what had felt like small daily installments that when assembled seemed like an enormous treasure. *Could there be a way to share this with others?* I wondered as I printed out the two pages and slipped the photograph back into the journal.

The next morning, I put on the vintage suit jacket that Joe had liked and stepped over to the mirror to adjust the sleeves. I tucked the two folded pages into the inside pocket and hoped the man who looked back was ready to share if the opportunity arose. "Don't hide," I said aloud as I turned from side to side in the mirror. "Don't hide what Joe was to you."

A smile curled across Lilly's face when I entered the kitchen. "Whoa, dude, what's with the style?" she asked with her usual morning jab. "Do you have some kind of Match or OkCupid date?"

I smirked back at her as I poured a second cup of coffee. Elliott kept his uncombed bedhead buried in an open sketchbook.

"Oh my god," she continued, clearly enjoying herself. "It's a brunch date, isn't it? What is it with you boomers and brunch?"

"First of all, I am *not* a boomer. I'm Gen X. Remember the whole 'inventing angst' conversation?" I countered. "And second, brunch is awesome."

"Oh, you've got angst *so* nailed," Lilly said with an approving nod.

"I wish it was brunch. I'm attending a funeral. My friend Joe passed away and I might be speaking about him today, so I want to look my best."

Lilly pursed her lips and toned down their usual morning banter. "Aw, I'm sorry. You look really nice, Dad," she said as she walked over to hug me. "He was special to you, wasn't he?"

"He was a real gift to me. He saved me when I was struggling after I lost my job," I said, enjoying the familiar feel of her small frame in my arms.

269

"I know," she said, stepping back toward the table and her cup of tea.

"Whoa, Joe died?" Elliott said, looking up from his drawing. "I'm sorry, Dad. That sucks. He came into your life right when you needed him most."

"You *were* a hot mess before Joe," Lilly said.

"Yes, I was," I conceded with some embarrassment. "I've been revisiting that time. Joe opened my eyes about how I could be a better version of myself."

"Like not being such a sad sack all the time?" Lilly joked.

"Well, in so many words, yes."

"Geez, read the room, Lilly," Elliott interjected. "I wish I could have met Joe," he said as he slipped his toes under the warm pug sleeping beneath the kitchen table.

"He always asked about you guys. He was interested in how I was doing for both," I said over the steaming cup. "He wanted me to be happy in all parts of my life."

Lilly cocked her head a bit to the right and looked at me for a few seconds. "Well, your sad-to-sack ratio has been super low lately. I think it's working."

"Sad-to-sack ratio," I chuckled. "Joe would have loved that."

"Will you have to talk about Joe today, like in front of a lot of people?" Elliott asked.

"I don't know," I said as I thought again about how many might come for Joe's service.

"Dude, speech class is the worst! I am *not* a fan of public speaking," Lilly said, shaking her head.

"I don't like it either, but sometimes we have to do things like that. There could be a lot of people there today," I said, hoping it would be true.

Elliott closed his sketchbook and looked up at me. "Joe was really old, wasn't he?"

"He was eighty-eight."

I could see that he was thinking about what to say next. "There was a time I couldn't imagine living to eighteen, let alone eighty-eight. That's a big number. Can you even think of being that old? I can't."

"You have a few years to figure it out," I said. "Just put that same creative energy into your life as you do those sketchbooks, and it will be amazing."

"Have you *seen* my sketchbooks recently?"

"I peek sometimes. Your art isn't easy, but it *is* amazing. Just remember that you can draw whatever you want. I don't know what you will come up with, but I know the world will need it. Don't hide—the world needs people strong enough to live creative lives on their own terms."

"Elliott, you would make the best eccentric uncle if I ever have kids," Lilly said. "I can just see you pulling up in a vintage car like some mystical goth time traveler ready to draft a tattoo idea or create bone art with them."

"I love that," Elliott laughed before faking a serious tone. "I would be honored to be your kids' 'mystical, goth, time-traveling uncle.'"

Lilly didn't return his laugh as she looked right at him. "I'm serious, dude. I am going to need a big brother. Eighty-eight years, I want eighty-eight years out of ya."

271

Elliott returned her stare and his smile faded as he seemed touched by her request. "Yeah, okay," he muttered.

Lilly leaned in and stuck her hand out. "Eighty-eight years, shake on it!"

Elliott laughed and swatted her hand away, but Lilly persisted with her hand out. "Eighty-eight years."

I watched as my son straightened in his chair and extended his hand to take Lilly's. "I'll give you ninety years!" he boasted. "I may be living in your basement with ten cats, but I will be there. It's a deal."

"Deal, dude," Lilly said, shaking his hand.

She held onto Elliott, and it reminded me of Joe holding my hand as he coached me to ask for what I wanted out loud. This was

Lilly coming forward with a heavy heart to ask out loud for what she wanted. I was so impressed with her, and my heart latched onto the vision of a long life for Elliott.

"I bet there are going to be tons of people there today. You just watch," Lilly stated with confidence as they both looked over at me. "You'll be glad you dressed up."

Her smile filled me with joy the same way Joe's always had. "I think it's working." I replayed her words in my head as I thought about the happiness I enjoyed now because of him. *Would Joe live on through the joy he'd fostered in others?*

I pulled into the empty church parking lot where Joe's service would start and parked my car near the back, well away from the three cars parked in front of the double front doors. I sat in the car and felt pinned to the seat by a heaviness that I couldn't quite explain. When I tried to imagine the people who might turn up for Joe in a few minutes, I envisioned accomplished, successful, fully-realized, confident, song-singing people who would be celebrating a man they treasured and revered—but I didn't feel like that. All I felt was loss and a vacancy in my life that would now be permanent. They would know him as a mentor, a teacher, a motivator, a legendary public speaker, but would any of them really know him? I ran my hand over the words in my pocket as I tried to identify the heaviness I felt. *Would any of them know the strength he could summon to help someone new? Would they know how he inspired people in every moment of his life? Would they know that he could rescue hopeless people and show them a way forward?*

I opened the car door and willed myself to walk through the church doors, where I saw several poster boards covered in photographs lining the entryway. Joe's smiling face looked out at me, and I couldn't help but smile back at my friend.

"Marcos," I heard a familiar voice call out from the hallway to my right. "You're early," said Judy, Joe's ex-wife.

"I thought you might need some help setting up," I said as I closed the distance to her until we were face-to-face in the hallway. "I'm so sorry about Joe."

"Me too," she said with a heavy sigh. "It was his time, Marcos. He started declining a few months ago and it didn't take him long to go."

"Can I help with anything?" I asked.

"Yes, you can. I am going to set up some snacks for after the memorial service. Can you help me bring them to the classroom next to the auditorium?"

"Sure," I said, eager to help her. "How many people do you think will come?"

"I sent out the announcement of Joe's passing to his list."

"His whole database?" I asked.

"Yes," she answered as she led me back out to her car. "I got with his last caregiver, and we just sent it to everyone."

"Judy, Joe had a lot of people on that list."

"We didn't count them. We just blasted it out," Judy said, handing me a covered aluminum tray filled with cookies.

"I prepared a few words to say about Joe if you need me to," I offered awkwardly. "I mean, if there isn't someone else—"

"I think a couple of Joe's most successful students are coming in to say a few words. I don't know what they prepared or how long they will go, but we have to have *some* public speakers for this, right?"

I chuckled as she loaded another tray on top. "Well, you can call on me if you need to today."

"Thanks, Marcos. He really treasured you; you know that, right?"

"He was very important to me."

"Joe always said you were one of the hard ones," she said with a smile as she held the church door open for me.

"I can see that," I laughed.

"When we finish setting up, can you go to the entrance and help direct everyone back to the auditorium?"

I paced the width of the lobby and counted down the long minutes until the first cars started to pull into the empty church parking lot. I didn't recognize the first middle-aged couple as I greeted them, but I did recognize the next two people who arrived together. It was the tall woman and the older man with the cane who had spoken about Joe at the Colorado Speakers Association meeting.

"Hello," I said to them both as they walked through the glass church doors.

"Hello," the woman replied. "You look familiar. Are you a public speaker?"

"No, I'm not a speaker or a student," I conceded as I extended my hand. "I was one of Joe's caregivers. I took him to a speakers' meeting and I think I met you there."

"I'm Joni," she said, shaking my hand firmly. "This is Gus."

"Thank you for taking care of my friend," Gus said, keeping his right hand tight on his cane's handle.

"He became my friend too. I'm so glad you came," I said. "You're one of the first ones here. We're gathering in the auditorium to the right."

Four younger women entered and promptly introduced themselves as students who had taken one of Joe's classes together and had stayed friends ever since. They were followed by a father and daughter who were also students. The girl had taken Joe's class and then talked her father into joining her to take it again.

Next, I heard a booming voice followed by laughter just beyond the glass doors and I turned to see Thomas, the chairman of the Colorado Speakers Association, flanked by two men in dark suits and four others surrounding them.

"Thomas," I said as I extended my hand toward him.

"Marcos," he bellowed before turning to both men in turn. "Gary, John, I want you to meet Marcos. He was one of those angels who took care of Joe in his final years." Thomas turned to me again and continued, "These two gentlemen are two of Joe's oldest students and they both canceled speaking engagements to fly in to deliver the eulogy for Joe."

"I am so pleased that you are speaking about Joe today. Joe talked about you both all the time, but especially in his classes. He was very proud of what you have accomplished."

John lowered his head and pursed his lips to keep his emotions in check. "Well, that didn't take very long," he said as he recovered.

"It could be an emotional morning," Gary said, putting his arm around John as they stepped toward the hallway.

I wandered around in the lobby and listened in on the conversations starting up about Joe as people looked at his photographs.

"He was such a great guy," Gus said.

"I hope I am that sharp in my eighties."

"We should make a new speaker award after him," an older woman offered.

"I hope I am working right up until the end like he did."

"I'm the speaker I am today because of him," a short woman said to her companion.

I wandered around the room feeling lost in the volley of accomplishments and appreciations. *Couldn't I have seen him just once more?* I thought as I listened to the accolades. *If only to reflect back to him what he had accomplished in me.*

"He helped me find my song," came a female voice from my left.

"Really, what's that?"

I listened to her answer, but it just raised more questions in me. *Am I doing all I can with the gifts Joe gave me? Am I singing loudly enough for others to hear me? Is this where it starts?*

I recognized the next man through the doors as Joe's podiatrist, Dr. Julian. "Hello, doctor."

"I remember you," he said, offering his hand. "You were one of Joe's drivers."

"Yes. And you were his favorite doctor," I said as I motioned him to the right toward the auditorium.

"I bet he told everyone that," he laughed.

I could see more people pulling into the parking lot as I paced, and I started to feel some relief that Joe would have a reasonable turnout. I searched for faces that I recognized as a crowd walked across the parking lot to the church doors. Steve, the Perkins manager, was next.

"Hi, Steve," I said with a wave.

"Hello," he answered and paused for a second. "Marcos, right?"

"Yes, how are things going at the restaurant?"

"Good, but I'm not the manager anymore; I run the region now. Twyla manages that store now. She said she will stop by."

"I miss going there with him," I said. "I think he was happiest during his lunches at Perkins."

"I miss him too," Steve started. "I didn't see him much in the past few months after I moved up. Joe was excited for me to take the promotion, but he sure did make it hard to leave. I told my new boss that I was spending most of my time at my old store to train Twyla, but it was really just to be around him a little longer," Steve said, choking up a bit. "I think I'll go inside now."

"Marcos!" came a shout from the crowd just beyond the doors. It was Marvin from the salon.

"Marvin, I'm so glad you could come."

"I flew in from Baltimore, but I wouldn't miss this for the world."

"Baltimore?"

"Yes, I quit at the salon and moved back home to follow through with finishing the nursing school plans that Joe and I talked about. I'm only two semesters from graduation now, and then I'll be singing my song as Maryland's newest nurse," he said with a flourish of his hand.

"Marvin, that's amazing. Joe would be so proud of you."

"I think you're right," Marvin agreed. "I'm proud of myself too. I picked up my spot and carried it all the way back to Maryland. Now let's go celebrate this man."

I turned back to the entrance and saw Patrick, the previous caregiver, walking toward me. "How are the dance moves coming?" he asked with a smile.

I took a dramatic ballroom step in his direction and then shook his hand. "I'm a bit out of practice now, but my old steps helped me steer Joe to safety a few times. I never did get the chance to dip him."

Patrick smiled. "How long were you with him?"

"I did the summer and early fall with him," I replied and noticed that he was without his wife. "Did you go and see him again?"

"Yeah, I went once. I wish I would have gone more often."

"I've been thinking that same thing, Patrick," I said.

"He knew we were just with him for a season," Patrick continued. "I feel like he always knew that he had a limited amount of time to work on us before we learned enough from him to take flight and be on our way."

I laughed at the bittersweet memory of stepping away from Joe to take the new job. "He knew when my time came."

"He was good that way. Hey, at least we can say we helped get him a little farther down his road," Patrick said.

THE NEXT GOOD THING

"I've been thinking about that too," I answered. "I hope you're right."

Twyla was next to arrive. Three of Joe's other favorite Perkins servers surrounded her and all four wore the trademark white Perkins dress shirts hidden under different blazers.

"I heard you're the manager now," I said to Twyla as they entered.

"Yes, Steve chose me, but it was Joe who showed me the way."

"We brought two of Joe's favorite pies," one of the servers said.

"Good," I said, taking the boxes from her. "There will be a reception after, and we'll need all the food we can get to feed this crowd."

"How are you?" Twyla asked. "I haven't seen you in a while. What are you up to?"

"I'm good," I replied as I thought about her second question. "I got my dream job," I said and realized it was the first time I had said it out loud.

"Well, that's two of us then."

I turned to address all four of them. "Well, if all of you are here, who is running the restaurant right now?"

"I left it in good hands," Twyla responded, "but the place does feel empty now without its mayor."

I nodded as I thought about Joe's booth sitting vacant at lunch today. "Come this way, we're gathering in here."

I waited at the entrance and greeted other friends, colleagues, and students whom Joe had collected and helped over the years.

When I finally followed the last people in, my heart swelled with the sight of an auditorium filled with people whom Joe had touched. Taking a seat near the back, I listened and laughed as Gary and then John recounted story after story about Joe. I smiled and ran my hand over my jacket pocket at hearing my own typed words from last night being spoken by other people who had received the same lessons from the same master. After their final words were spoken, I helped direct people to the reception, where I joined in a conversation with four people I didn't know.

I resolved to tell my story last as I asked each one in turn, "How did you know Joe?"

"Joe came to me for physical therapy," the first woman said. "I was still working as a therapist while I was studying acupuncture and traditional Asian remedies. Joe insisted that I practice on him." She laughed. "'Give me the needles,' he used to say to me.

"Joe saw that I had a passion for Eastern medicine," she continued with a smile. "We were together for two years, but I think he worked more on me than I did on him. He transformed my life."

"That sounds about right," a man in his mid-forties chimed in. "I met Joe through one of his courses. He helped me find *both* of my songs."

"Two songs?" I asked.

"Yes, I became a teacher because of Joe. I teach elementary kids. I adore it. The world is new to them, and their curiosity really jazzes me. I also write books, kids' books, about climate change and the difference all of us can make. And besides, no one ever said we couldn't have more than one song," he concluded.

"My song is the other way around," said the second man in our group, a tall, lanky man with a cheerful face. "I was a science teacher, and I was miserable. Joe showed me that your song could be anything, even something like being a wedding planner."

"Science to weddings?" asked the older woman standing next to me.

"Yes. I know it sounds crazy, but I've never been happier," the man beamed as he looked at her. "Imagine a job where you make it possible for people to enjoy the happiest day of their lives. It's magic, pure magic—every time.

"What about you?" he asked, turning the question back to her.

"I met Joe through my late husband. After Paul passed, Joe started calling more to check in on me," she started as she wove a hand through her thick gray hair. "He started in with these crazy questions like: What excited me? What were my passions? What made me want to get out of bed in the morning?

"At first I thought it was pure nonsense," she continued. "But he didn't stop. I don't think Joe ever stopped," she said in time with everyone's laughter. "The more I thought about it, the more I wanted to go back to college and finish my degree. It was madness. But there I was, recently widowed, had just turned sixty, and hadn't been in a classroom in nearly forty years. Oh god, I felt so out of place," she said as she placed her hand on my arm. "I was twenty years older than all my professors. I got some stares, that's for sure."

"And?" I asked, prompting her to finish.

"And"—she smiled—"I received my degree four years ago. I'm a freelance writer now. In some ways, I feel like I am just getting started."

New people joined our circle with more stories about Joe and how he had changed their lives. And as I listened, I realized that my inspirational story was just one of many and that I was surrounded by Joe's Songs. And it was then that I knew I had to raise my voice so that others could hear mine.

Concentrating on the stories around me, I closed my eyes and saw a vision of Joe holding my hand just as we had walked together hundreds of times. But then Joe let go and stepped away from me. I smiled as my old friend released his fancy cane and let it drop to the floor. I kept the wonderful image of him in my mind as I watched Joe slowly unfold his clenched arm and start flexing a reawakening leg as though beginning a dance.

"That's a great story," I said loud enough to be heard over the other conversations in the room. "Let me tell you about my time with Joe."

Acknowledgments

The authors would like to acknowledge David Fugate at Launch-Books for finding a wonderful home for this book.

The authors would also like to acknowledge the wonderful team at Union Square who helped us tell this story:

Barbara Berger, executive editor

Alison Skrabek, project editor

Lisa Forde, creative director

Elizabeth Lindy, cover designer

Kevin Ullrich, interior designer

Sandy Noman, production manager

Diana João, copyeditor

A Conversation with Marcos Perez

Did you ever have any doubts about following the guidance of doing the next good thing while you were with Joe?

I didn't. It was kind of a compelling sort of thing. I remember everything else felt so bad in my life, and there was this one thing that felt good. So even though it didn't make any sense, I only had one good thing in front of me and I was like, "Yes, I'll have one good thing." "Okay, I'll be doing one good thing. And so, I'll just do that." I remember feeling like that was what I *could* do. And that started this whole thing.

How would you advise people who might be struggling in life to use Joe's lessons like you did?

That's the big question. I would say to read each one of the lessons in the book slowly and let it unfold, because that's just kind of how it worked with Joe and me. Open your heart to it, and just let it lead you and work for you. And remember to "Ask for It."

Which of Joe's ten lessons has been most valuable to you?

[Laughing] Oh, the one I'm working on right now.

It would have to be "Pick Up Your Spot and Move It." I am spending a lot of my time right now on work-focused items, and they could easily consume me or overwhelm me, but I have to realize that work is just a place I visit and remember that I am Marcos, and my life is good. I love my kids, I love my house, I love my life. Knowing that work and life occupy different spots on the map is key to knowing your way home at the end of the day.

How do you think Joe's lessons prepared you to be the dad that Elliott needed?

At the time, I think I was getting too involved in the problem of Elliott—like the scariness of it all, the suicidal thoughts and actions. It was terrifying and I got really wrapped up in that. Joe's thing was to take a step back and see what you have so you're not affected by your fear of the situation. Joe helped me to see my son outside of my fears, and that showed me a positive point of view that made me recognize, "Yes! This is exactly what I want for myself and my kid." I think that gave him the space to become the young man that he is today.

Do you feel like your time with Joe, or even writing this book about your time with him, helped you find your song?

Yes, 100 percent. Just by working through the notes from my time with Joe, I had to relive his lessons. So when I wrote them out it was like receiving them all over again. The lesson that struck me the most was "Ask for It." That immediately brought me back to asking for it in the car with Joe. Since that day, I have been working toward my song of becoming a therapist to work with kids like Elliott.

How do you think Joe would feel about his time with you being captured in a book?

Well, he *did* ask me to write about this on social media, and I never went back to do it after I lost the original file. I think he really wanted to see me write down the progress he thought he was achieving with me. I know I wasn't one of the easy ones for Joe. He wanted his efforts to resonate with me, to realize what I was getting from him, that I was changing. I see it so clearly now.

287

I think Joe's view of the book would be that it's a good thing it is out in the world now. That was *his* song, and now I get to keep it alive through this book. And I think he would be proud of me.

If you could have five more minutes with Joe, what would you tell him?

I would just blubber. It would be a lot of blubbering. I would thank him. He invested a lot in me, but in the end, I realized he did that with everyone. What an inspirational mission he was on. I would tell him how much he inspired and helped me.

Book Club Questions
for Discussion

1. Do you think you would have followed the "just do the next good thing" guidance that Marcos received (and taken a low-paying job you weren't qualified for)?

2. Do you think his decision to follow that guidance was brave and inspiring?

3. What was your favorite scene from the book? What lesson did it hold for you?

4. Did you have a favorite "Joe lesson" in the book? Why did it appeal to you?

5. Do you have someone like Elliott in your life? If so, how do you think the lessons in this book could help them?

6. If you had the chance to ask Marcos Perez one question, what would it be?

7. Who are the people in your life you would like to share this book with?